AWAY WITH WORDS

HOW YOU CAN LEARN ANY LANGUAGE & CULTIVATE AN IDIOMATIC MINDSET

RYAN DOHERTY

CONTENTS

This, my first book, is dedicated to the teachers and professors, classmates and colleagues I've met and befriended. Also to my parents, my sister and my beautiful wife and children, who have supported me and enthralled me with their language learning capabilities over the years. Also to our two dogs, Benji and Shadow and the cats, mousers extraordinaire - Sansa & Cosmo!

Written by Ryan Doherty

various sources. Please consult a licensed professional before attempting any techniques outlined in this book.

By reading this document, the reader agrees that under no circumstances is the author responsible for any losses, direct or indirect, which are incurred as a result of the use of the information contained within this document, including, but not limited to, — errors, omissions, or inaccuracies.

A FREE GIFT FOR MY READERS

Included with your purchase of this book is the Language Learner's Checklist: The 7 most important things you need to know to learn a language quickly.

This checklist will give you hints and tips to get your language learning off to the best start. Click the link below and let us know which email address to deliver it to:
7stepchecklist.ryandohertybooks.com

INTRODUCTION

If you were anything like me at school, you HATED languages. Lists of verb conjugations, pronouns, tenses... What was the point of it all? In fact, if you were anything like me, you probably hated most lessons. It's not that I wasn't good at them. I wasn't brilliant; I wasn't a prodigy. Probably the best term for me was 'average'. While I wasn't the worst, I was far from the best. One term that generally seems to have fit me well is "jack of all trades, master of none", or as the Spanish say: "aprendiz de todo, maestro de nada".

So how did I end up speaking over five languages fluently? In this book, you will find out! You will also discover how changing my mindset changed everything. Indeed, changing your mindset is one of the most powerful things you can do to achieve anything worthwhile in life.

In this book you will discover:

- Why you think learning a language is difficult.
- How children learn languages so easily.
- How to go about learning a language.
- 5 proven ways you can build your language knowledge.
- The best way to get vocab into your long term memory.
- Why learning a language is actually fun. (Sometimes rib-crackingly hysterical!)
- How to become aware of your language.
- How I learned to speak Italian in 1 week!

WHY YOU THINK LEARNING A LANGUAGE IS DIFFICULT.

The major problem I see with people learning languages starts at school. It's taught wrongly and because it's taught wrongly to us as children, what we actually learn in language classes is that it's HARD!

My son was born in Barcelona. We spoke Spanish at home, his mother being Spanish, and he spoke Catalan at school. Later, due to my work, we moved to the Flemish part of Belgium when he was around six or seven, where he attended a normal Dutch-speaking school. He said it was like listening to Chinese when he first got there, but kids are kids and within a few weeks he was already speaking Dutch fluently if not perfectly and had made a lot of friends. It's very strange, a little demoralizing, but ultimately fascinating to see your little boy acquire a new language within just a few days when you've spent years at it. Two years passed and I was moved again, this time to the UK where my son was enrolled in the local 'middle' school. By now he spoke fluent Catalan, Spanish and Dutch, but I hadn't spoken to him in English, despite it being my mother tongue, for fear of overloading the poor tyke.

Again within a few days he managed to convert a lot of his Dutch, which is very similar to English in many ways, and muddled together a grasp of conversational English. He made new friends at school and in just a few weeks more, I was unable to tell from his accent that he hadn't been born here.

It was in his second year at that middle school that the language teaching problem became glaringly apparent. We were invited to his second parents' evening, where we had the opportunity to discuss his progress with his French teacher.

'Lee works very hard', she informed us, 'but his French is very poor and he seems to really struggle with language learning'.

Needless to say, I was both shocked and amazed. How could this have happened? The little guy was now only ten and was fluent in four languages, but according to the earnest teacher sitting across the desk from us his French was abysmal. I was taken aback for a few seconds, before deciding to tackle this view-point head on.

'What do you think of Lee's English?' I asked her. She looked a bit confused. She'd joined the school at the start of term and didn't know of my son's initial lack of English a year previously. 'His English?' She stuttered. 'His English is fine, why?'

'Because he didn't speak it 2 years ago', I replied. I went on to inform her that the little boy she was worried didn't have the wherewithal for French already spoke perfect Spanish, Catalan and Dutch, and his seemingly native English had been picked up just in the last two years from scratch. If there is anything at all wrong with his French, I informed her, it was definitely the fault of the teacher and not the student.

In retrospect, I regret saying this. It wasn't her fault either - she was just following the curriculum as she had been taught it. But obviously a child can learn a language in a few weeks, there's no denying this, so why employ methods that :

- Don't work
- Are boring
- Are totally useless or, worse, detrimental
- Build a deep aversion to learning languages later in life

My answer is: I'm not sure. I don't know why language courses are built this way. I can only assume the logic goes something like this:

Most languages are something like 90% similar. Even totally diverse languages from different language groups share elements of grammar and syntax. There are numbers to count with, words for colours, adjectives to describe things and ways of explaining who is doing what to whom and when.

Take languages from the same language tree, (English and German, for example or Spanish and Portuguese) and the similarities strengthen and become more numerous.

And so what's the fastest way to learn them? Point out the differences between them!

The only drawback to this method of course, as we have already posited, is that it doesn't work without context and therefore probably shouldn't be used until much later in the language learning process. Not till the passion has been built, the ability to communicate is there, and the aim shifts from speaking to perfecting.

Most people once they get good at something can make the shift to wanting to be the best at something. But if you take someone who's never done an activity before, for example running a marathon or doing the high jump, and you set the bar in that first lesson at the Guinness world records for those disciplines, it isn't going to be motivating. Neither is it helpful. Rather than making learning a language a joy, this method just presents it as years and years of problems to overcome.

The common outlook when embarking on the task of learning a language is that you will have months and months of reading lists of words off a page, trying to desperately memorise them, only to realise days later you can't recall 90% of them. Having to read pages of verb conjugations, with no real idea of what they are for or why they need to be used, textbooks with childish cartoons of Tom and Sally asking each other where they come from and would they like a cup of coffee? What you'd much rather be able to do is have a conversation about your favourite hobby or be able to use your language for job-related events or to meet that special someone.

HOW CHILDREN LEARN LANGUAGES SO EASILY.

S o how did my son manage to learn four languages before he was a teenager?

I'm no psychologist but I can make a few observations. He didn't learn by studying, for one. He learnt primarily by listening, copying and living in the language. One of my favourite quotes is:

> He who has a why to live for can bear almost any how.

— FRIEDRICH NIETZSCHE

My son had his WHY clearly, albeit subconsciously, worked out. He desperately wanted to fit in, make new friends, and more importantly, HAVE FUN! He wasn't worried about making mistakes, he didn't concern himself with grammar, he wasn't embarrassed by his "foreign accent". Or maybe he was to some degree, but what's certain is that his primary goal, his entire focus, was being able to play with his new friends.

When his friends spoke, he listened carefully. When they didn't understand each other they pointed, drew pictures and laughed with glee when they managed to get their points across, all while playing hide and seek, football or card games. I see a lot of experts discussing language acquisition in children and marvelling about their plastic brains and everything that goes in their favour. However, adults also have plasticity in the brain, the capacity to create new neural networks. What adults also carry, which most children generally don't take to language learning, is baggage and negativity.

The truth is anyone can learn a language - even you! You've already done so or you wouldn't be able to read this book. And you can do it again! You can also learn to learn, which means that as you learn, your brain remembers how to learn and the process speeds up exponentially as you continue. You just need to be clear about why you want to do it and remember that that "why" is more important than the idea of giving up. It needs to be fun, and it needs to be related to what interests you in in real life.

HOW TO GO ABOUT LEARNING A LANGUAGE.

*I*n my opinion, the best way to go about learning your first foreign language is two-fold.

Firstly, immerse yourself in the language as much as possible from day one. There's a saying that comes up again and again when meeting other polyglots: 'The best way to learn a language is in the bedroom'. When you meet people that speak several languages, they quite often have or have had a foreign partner. You of course don't literally learn in the bedroom, but it does describe quite nicely the relationship between success and immersion. You have to commit 100% to learning the language, as you would commit to a relationship, and when you begin a literal relationship with someone that speaks a different language to yourself, you also commit to learning not only all about that language but also about the culture. Your passion and love for your partner also becomes a passion for their language, culture and even their cuisine. The circle is complete, your motivation is at its maximum. Language learning becomes easy, fun, and reinforces your relationship.

Now I'm not suggesting you run out and find someone who speaks the language you want to learn and ask them out on a date (though it might not be the worst thing you could do). What I am suggesting is that you commit and immerse yourself immediately.

Secondly, learn your native language! If this is English, you're in a great position! English is quite a unique language due to several quirks of history. Its grammar is 90% Germanic, whilst I believe something like 70% of its vocabulary is Latin based, coming either directly from Latin during the Roman Occupation of Britain or via old French from the Norman Invasion of 1066.

Ever wondered why meat and the animals they come from are named differently? The answer is the Norman Conquest. That fateful day Harold received an arrow to the eye for his troubles changed English forever. The new rulers spoke Old French, the peasants Old English. The people raising the meat spoke Old English and referred to the animals as pigs and cows, while the rulers who predominantly ate that meat called it pork (porc) and beef (boef). Modern English is a great language to start learning other European languages from, particularly as most European languages stem from either a Germanic or Latin ancestor and English comes from both. If you can learn to spot the difference you can use it to your advantage!

Here are a few examples:

Anglo-Saxon / Old French

- Thoughtful / Pensive
- Motherly / Maternal
- Ask / Enquire
- Ghost / Phantom
- Hunt / Chase
- Freedom / Liberty

If you're learning a Germanic language (English, Dutch, German, Danish, etc) and you're looking for a word to describe a spooky figure, you'd do well to think of the Anglo-Saxon term 'ghost' and you could hit upon *geist* in German. Talking of spooky, 'ghost' in Dutch is *sprookje*, which is where 'spooky' comes from, or rather, they share a common root word. If you're learning a Romance language (Spanish, Italian, French, Portuguese, etc) it would be better to think of the Latin term phantom to get to Spanish *fantasma* for example or *fantôme in French*. Which words come from which language tree is actually quite easy to spot as you start learning another European language. Especially if you learn one Germanic language and one Romance language, you'll pick up the feel for it without trying.

One major reason people fail when learning their first foreign language is their lack of knowledge about their mother tongue! This was my experience when learning German. I was studying A-level German at college (which is pre-university level in England). We leave school at 16, do normally two years of college and those A-levels are what get us into University where we can study to degree level. Anyway, German is one of a few languages that use a case system to denote who is doing what to whom. Other examples of languages that use cases would be Latin and Finnish.

To understand cases, you need to understand sentence structure. Clearly, neither myself nor the rest of my class understood sentence structure at all! After nearly three months of trying to drum the German case system into her dim-witted class and failing miserably, our teacher was no closer to seeing us grasp the Teutonic brainteaser that was cases.

Exasperated, she ranted for ten minutes on the state of the education system in Britain and how could we not, in our second year of college, distinguish a subject from an indirect object? She announced there and then that all German classes were cancelled and for the next two weeks minimum we would be studying English grammar only. We all groaned and held our heads in our hands. Honestly? It was the best thing I ever did (or had done to me) and I think it was one of the top things that sent me on my path to being a successful polyglot.

It's practically impossible to learn a language without coming across terms such as 'adverb', 'present participle', 'object', 'passive voice'. It can be quite easy to skip past them, as the words are mostly commonplace. 'Present' is a word you know, so is 'participle'. A present participle? Well, it can't be that important, let's carry on reading! This is a fatal error. These are terms for the building blocks of language. If you understand what they refer to, how to use them, where they come from and how they relate to English, you are armed with information that can help you conquer any language. How can you talk about something in the future in Spanish, if you don't know how to build the future tense in English? How can you understand who is doing what to whom in German if you can't point out the subject of a sentence in English? The answer is you can't! Understanding and learning English is fundamental to understanding another language.

This is such easy stuff to learn as well. It's definitely not rocket science, but I don't see it being taught as part of any language course, at least when it comes to formal education.

I'd highly advise you look up these terms as you come across them and make sure you fully understand how they work in English before trying to apply them to your target language. The good thing is, once you do understand them, learning multiple other languages suddenly becomes incredibly simple (as you'll find out soon when I describe how I learned to speak Italian in one week!) A secondary consequence of this is you will become a better speaker, a better writer, and a better thinker, able to pick up invaluable insights as you listen to how other people build their sentences sometimes revealing subtle motives or evasions of truth.

This is obviously a tantalising place to conclude. However, I'm not a cruel man so allow me to elaborate in the next chapter.

A BRIEF LESSON IN ENGLISH GRAMMAR.

*I*n this chapter we will cover the bare basics of English Grammar. Don't panic if you hate grammar, just try and follow along I've made it as easy as possible.

A sentence can be built from a subject and an object. The object can be direct or indirect. The person doing the verb (or "doing word", eg. to swim, to play, to sing, to jump, etc) is the subject.

The man sings. Who sings? The man, so he is the subject of this sentence.

The girl jumps. Who jumps? The girl, so she is the subject of this sentence.

A dog barks. Who barks? The dog, so it is the subject of this sentence.

The object is direct if it is the direct recipient of the action.

The man sings a song. What did he sing ? A song, so the song is the direct object.

The dog barked at the man . Who did it bark at? The man, so the man is the direct object.

An indirect object is not directly affected by the subject.

The man (subject) gave the ball (direct object) to the girl (indirect object).

Note the fact that in English the indirect object is marked by the word 'to'.

In German or Latin, this would be handled slightly differently. Some languages add "bits" or suffixes to the ends of words to note this function. This would be a bit like us adding bits on the ends of English words to create a different meaning. There are a few examples of this I can think of:

How big was the chicken? 'It was fairly big' vs. 'it was big<u>ish</u>'. See how we can add 'ish' to the end of 'big' to introduce some doubt or vagueness without an extra word?

Or another example ... What colour was her dress? 'It was a kind of yellowy colour'. Here we added 'y' which is quite often added to colours to reduce the certainty of the hue. This adding endings onto words is much more common in other languages than it is in English but it's a really beautiful and useful feature.

We have some leftovers in English of adjectival endings that mark words. For example, a spoon made of wood is a wooden spoon and the goose laid a golden egg. If you study German you will learn that it is these adjectival endings that help mark subjects and objects.

Going back to our sentence about the ball, one could ask: 'to whom, did the man give the ball?' or 'who did the man give the ball to?'

The who/whom variation is to do with old case markers that dropped away in modern English, but it's still nice to see these "leftovers" and understand what they are doing. It's another way of solving the same problem of working out who is doing what to who(m).

But why do we *need* to work it out? It depends on how any particular language is built. There are two common options: either have a fixed word order, which English kind of has, or you can have a completely flexible word order, but then case needs to be marked.

For example, look at the English sentence:

'The woman gave the baby to the man.'

The subject usually goes first, followed by the verb, and then the direct object. The indirect object is marked by 'to'.

As English uses a fixed structure, the meaning changes if I rearrange the words.

The baby gave the woman to the man, does not have the same meaning as *the woman gave the baby to the man*.

But because the indirect object is marked, we can play with that and keep the meaning the same.

To the man, the woman gave the baby.

You see, we changed the word order here, but because the indirect object is marked you still got the same meaning as the first sentence (albeit it seems a bit more clumsy or archaic). So what about a language that puts the verb at the end of the sentence?

The baby the man the woman gave.

Here as nothing is marked we now have no idea who is giving what to whom. Is it the woman giving the baby to the man, or the man giving the woman to the baby? I hope this illustrates how cases work or what they are coding.

In Latin or Finnish for example where all cases are marked, you could pretty much swap around the sentence order as much as you please and the same meaning will always be understood. This was also how Old English worked but as the case system and its endings dropped out of use, the word order became much more fixed to compensate.

This brings us to the passive voice. The passive voice can be used quite sneakily, sometimes innocently and sometimes psychopathically. It's good to be able to spot it and question why it is being used.

Most sentences have a subject, as we have seen above, and are referred to as being written in the 'active voice'. However, it is also possible to create a sentence without a subject, which effectively means we're omitting stating who is doing the action.

Active sentence: 'The <u>dog</u> bit the man.' (the subject is dog)

Passive sentence: 'The man was bitten… (by whom?)

In the first sentence, we know who the culprit is and who isn't getting a bone for his supper. In the second example, we know the outcome of the action, but the culprit is left in doubt.

A common cry from upset children who have just knocked over Mummy's favourite vase is 'it got knocked over!', which uses an instinctive and sneaky trick of grammar to eliminate the culprit behind the fine rubble on the floor. Recognising this type of sentence structure can tell you a lot, not just about what people are telling you, but also what they are studiously trying to *avoid* telling you! And once you know how to distinguish between the passive voice and active voice in English, it's a five minute job to learn it in another language. I hope this piques your interest in grammar, which is not a set of boring rules but something that provides you with a huge amount of information about a sentence. You get so much of this intuitively as a native speaker, but if you can consciously parse or build a sentence with a good grasp of grammar all sorts of wonderful insights and clues can be retrieved or embedded into the words.

FIVE PROVEN WAYS YOU CAN BUILD YOUR LANGUAGE KNOWLEDGE.

1. THE INTERNET IS YOUR FRIEND

*S*earch for a local radio station in the target language on google. These days you can listen to radio anywhere in the world online for free! Try and find a radio station that plays the music you like or discusses the topics you're interested in. You can even download apps that allow you to play internet radio on your smartphone. Have it on all day in the background at home or at work if you can, even doing the daily commute.

Do the same with television. After all, there are a wide array of channels you can view online from around the world. Watch your favourite movie or series and switch the audio to the target language and put subtitles on. 'What? From day one?!' I hear you cry. Yes! Yes! Yes!

You won't understand a word, I know, but that's irrelevant. Your brain will automatically try to make sense of it. Don't try to - just leave your brain to do what it does best. Subconscious learning happens without you even knowing it. Driving to work listening to Spanish radio, or a Japanese news channel, your brain will be picking up on interesting phonemes, registering patterns, noting rhythms and pauses, spotting sounds that repeat often, even picking up on words it recognizes. Don't try to understand, but rather let the experience wash over you. Another important thing is to enjoy the *not*-understanding. This may sound strange, but firstly it takes the requirement off you to do anything or reach any goal - your goal is just to simply experience it. This means you can do it continually, every day all day, and it won't be frustrating which means there's no reason to stop! Secondly, part of the reason you want to learn is precisely because you don't understand, right? Enjoy the journey, find pleasure in the process. Soon you will understand. It's like tuning in to a radio station: at first there's static and mumbling, but gradually the signal becomes clearer in your brain and then you suddenly realise you do understand. I can't remember how it felt to not understand the languages I speak but I still get that sense of excitement when I hear someone speaking one I don't know!

2. WAX LYRICAL

If you take me up on the internet radio suggestion, at some point you're going to come across a song you fall in love with. One of the best things about learning languages is exposing yourself to non-English music. New singers and bands you'd never heard of making the music you love! It's very exciting to come across an amazing new band and think, 'If I'd never started learning x language I'd never have all this great music to listen to!' It's also a great way to improve your vocabulary, build up speed pronouncing the words (which may involve moving your lips and tongue into positions you're not used to, so prepare for some numbness) and learn chunks of sentences and turns of phrase which you can steal directly and use for yourself.

A great thing to do is get the lyrics to your favourite song in your target language and look up all the words. It's your favourite song and you're excited to know what they are singing about! This shouldn't feel like a chore. It's getting to know a fantastic new group or singer. This is the mindset! Everything is passion and fun. Once you have all the words you didn't know looked up, start trying to translate the song. If you get stuck, ask someone online. Join a Facebook group or find a language club. There's no excuse these days - the whole world is connected!

Having translated and learned your song, you can now sing along with it when it comes on. This builds retention. The more you listen to it - it is your favourite song after all - the more all that vocab, grammar, and pronunciation is going to get into your head. I can't recommend this activity enough. It's fun and highly effective. Make sure you sing along!

3. YOUR ADVANTAGE

Once you have a basic vocabulary and a basic grasp of grammar (at least in the present tense), start making up simple conversations in your head. I know this may sound nuts - and maybe I'm a bit nuts - but it worked for me. Make sure you start in English and make the sentences as simple as possible. Remember you speak English fluently, so use it to your advantage and adapt your sentences so it's easy to translate. The aim here is to be able to say whatever you want as simply as possible.

For example, you might start off with a 'Hi mate/buddy, how're you doing? Have you got the time on you?'

Try and spot if you're using slang and get rid of it. Try and understand what you're actually asking and see if there is an easier way to render it.

Hi mate/buddy, is going to be simplified as 'Hello friend'. I know we don't speak like this in English, but we're not trying to speak English - we're trying to speak a foreign language, so get it down to its most basic form.

'Have you got the time on you?' - would be better written as 'what is the time'?

Usually when it comes to sentence length, the shorter the better.

A lot of initial problems people have trying to speak or write in a foreign language come from the fact that they want to translate native-level English with beginners'-level Spanish or French or whatever language they're learning and it's just not possible at first. Your advantage is your native English. You know how to simplify it. So work on playing with your English. Make your translations easier. Get used to thinking this way in your head all the time.

The quicker you can rework your English into basic sentences and have it become second nature, the more brain power and time you have to think of the vocab you need for the translation. You should, with practice, be making up small sentences within a few hours, and you will find that most conversations run around the same themes. You have the interests that you like talking about so think of words that relate to that and look them up. Once you can quickly rework what you're actually thinking in English to a basic short sentence and translate it, you're actually halfway along the road to becoming fluent. Eventually, you will do it so quickly you will be able to chat away quite easily, albeit at a very basic level. This is when the magic starts to happen. The more you converse and use the language, the more you learn.

This is the secret to language learning. The learning accelerates massively once you are at the chatting stage. One reason for this is that even if there's a word you don't know you can usually find a way to describe. If you don't know the word 'glass' but you know the word 'window', you can ask 'what are windows made from?' and you just learned a new word. Now if you want it to go into your long term memory, start using it in sentences! Do this however you want. I was quite happy to make a fool of myself and just blurt out ten random sentences using a word I'd just learned with my interlocutor looking at me like I was from Mars and had just got out of my flying saucer, but using vocab is the only way to get it into your long term memory. How many times have you learned a list of 20 words for a test and two days later you can only remember one or two of them? Memorising words from lists just puts them into your short term memory. You can't fool your brain: it's not going to go to all the trouble of building a new neural path for nothing. When you use words constantly, your brain correctly assumes it's worth the trouble and drops them into your long term memory.

The second reason your learning accelerates is that the person you're talking with, if they are a fluent speaker, is going to say things that you understand but would never have thought to say in that particular way. Make a mental note when this happens! Try and write it down if you can, or if it's a friend ask them to say it again and record it on your phone. And again, use it! Try to use other vocab to build similar sentences. This is yet another great thing about language learning: people express themselves differently in other languages. Ok, it makes it a little bit more difficult to learn at times, but ultimately once you have imbibed it and made it your own you're now able to express yourself differently and think about things with an entirely new set of tools. This is incredibly freeing and exciting!

4. ETYMOLOGY

This is the study of the origin of words, and a great way of learning a new language is learning where the words you use on a daily basis come from. Languages from quite disparate language groups quite often evolve along surprisingly similar routes, and if you know what they are it can be a fun game to guess what certain words would look like in another language. You'd be surprised how often you can get it right. Even funnier is when the word guessed at actually exists but means something completely different. If you're learning a European language this is even more beneficial as it links back to what we spoke of earlier regarding recognising which English words you use come from Latin and which are Germanic.

I'll always remember my Spanish friend who'd come to the UK in the winter and, wanting to tell me he felt frozen, tried to translate the Spanish word *helado* from the verb helar (to freeze). Note that in Spanish, the 'h' isn't pronounced when it's used at the start of a word. Therefore, *helado* would be pronounced as "elado". He took a chance, guessed the verb might exist in English and told me he was "elated".

I was surprised and impressed. Firstly, he didn't look elated but actually looked pretty miserable, huffing and puffing in the cold, wearing a huge coat and scarf, and rubbing his hands together. His grasp of English was usually rudimentary so where he'd got this gem of vocabulary from I didn't know, but 10 out of 10 for using it! I was a fan of his method!

I did ask 'Go on then, why are you elated?' and it was his turn for surprise. He switched back to Spanish and told me: *Pues hace un frío que me cago tío!* Not an easy sentence to translate back to English, but essentially he wasn't too impressed with the temperature and as he watched me reverse engineer his sentence to work out where I'd gone wrong in parsing it, I suddenly worked out what he'd done and we both burst out laughing at the same time. Being a linguist though I couldn't let it go and explained to him that 'elated' does exist in English but means you're extremely happy about something and advised him to use it when he wanted to show off with his vocabulary.

An interesting example of etymology is the story of why we say 'hello' when we meet people, what that has to do with the verb "to holler" (or to shout to someone) and the possibility that these words are directly related to Spanish Hola - meaning 'hello'...

Originally there probably wasn't a formal word with the function of acknowledging meeting someone. There would have been some kind of exchange along the lines of 'Wes hal' with wes being an imperative form of the Old English verb *wesen* meaning 'to be' (learners of German should recognise the word 'Wesen' as meaning 'being' or 'creature' from the same root) and *hal* signifying health. So *wes hal* could literally translated to "be well" or something along those lines. We shouldn't analyse this as a greeting though. At the time I would expect it was thought of as a serious wish of good health, rather than just a precursor to the start of a conversation as we use 'hello' today.

The story goes something like this... Most towns and cities sprung up around rivers for obvious reasons. Cities would have grown on both sides of the river and the handiest way to get from one side to the other was via boat. A quick check on Google shows there's a fair bit of argument about when bridges were first built, what constitutes a bridge and which the oldest is. I think, however, it's safe to say that only the richest and most populous cities would have had bridges, and initially on the larger rivers. The boatman was probably quite a popular chap!

What happens though when you wander down to the river, hoping to trade some goods on the other side, or visit a friend and the river-faring freelancer is nowhere to be seen? You'd likely surmise, as he isn't Phileas Fogg, that he hasn't set sail to circumnavigate the globe. Rather, he's probably on the other side of the river having dropped off another fare, and hoping for a repeat. As an interesting aside, 'fare' is related to the German verb 'fahren' (to travel). 'Fahren' also lingers on in English as the word 'farewell' meaning 'goodbye', which would have literally meant 'travel well'. As another aside (I can't help myself), 'goodbye' is actually a corruption of 'God be with you' which became just 'God be' and then, probably during the Great Vowel Shift of the 1600s (though I could be wrong about this), the vowel sounds changed. People had forgotten the original meaning, 'God' was confused with 'good', and 'be' became 'bye' obscuring the original meaning further still. This is quite common and personally I find it fascinating delving into our language's past to learn how it all came about.

Back to our story. So the boatman is sitting on the other side of the river waiting for a fare, whilst our intrepid travellers are stuck over on the opposite bank. How do they get him to pick them up? Back in the day, they wouldn't have had much choice but to yell at the top of their lungs and depending on the breadth of the river, hope their voices would travel and he'd hear them. According to the Oxford English Dictionary, the word they shouted would have been something like *halâ* or *holà* which came from Old High German and was the imperative form (meaning to give an order) of the verb 'to fetch'.

'Halâ'/'holà' became 'hallo/hollo' and still is 'hallo' today in Germany. It became 'hello' in English and I suspect is the origin of the Spanish word 'hola'. This seems to be somewhat debated. However it is said that the name of the southern Spanish region of

Andalucia derives from the Vandals - a Germanic tribe that travelled south to the Iberian peninsula - and would have originally started life as something like Vandalucia.

This is a good example of a word splitting and ending up with two separate meanings within the same language, and tying it all back together is one of the most satisfying things to achieve. Over time shouting to the boatman to come and fetch you, especially on some of the smaller rivers, would have shifted in connotation from a request to a greeting as the original meaning of the word became lost in time. But it would have also been reinterpreted as the other thing that was happening: that being all the yelling going on. So 'holler' became a verb meaning to shout and 'hello' became a greeting, though - unless you're interested in languages and etymology - you wouldn't suspect they had anything to do with each other.

5. MNEMONICS

These are basically any learning technique that helps you remember information. If you want to remember vocabulary easily there are two things you can do. The first one is something we've already talked about: learn a word and use it! Use it often, and if you haven't got any reason to use it, make one up. Form sentences in your mind, write some down or put stickers on your fridge. The second method is mnemonics. If you utilise the two together it is immensely powerful and you will quickly build a vast vocabulary that you will be able to access on demand and without stalling. The more work you put into this, the quicker and more vivid the recall will be.

So how do mnemonics work? My son came to me a few months back and excitedly announced he would be learning Japanese. He was now 18 and for the first time was going to try and learn a language as an adult. He had an interest in manga (Japanese comic books) and decided it would be cool to read them in the original language. He looked up how to count to 10 and proudly showed his mum and I that he was able do it. We never heard about Japanese again. After a week or so I decided to ask him about it. 'How's your Japanese going Lee?' 'Mmm' was the only reply I got. I tried again: 'do you still remember how to count to 10?' The answer was 'no' and came with the distinct insinuation that this wasn't a topic he wanted to dwell on. What had happened to my little language learning prodigy of old? He'd learned four languages fluently to mother tongue ability and at 18 he couldn't retain how to count up to 10?

He'd hit the brick wall of adulthood and nothing would be the same again. Only joking! He just wasn't employing the same mindset and tactics that he had done unconsciously in his youth. This is after all part of what becoming an adult is: becoming conscious of why things are done a certain way and building awareness of the world around us so we can conduct ourselves in it in a beneficial and harmonious way. I myself can see how as a teenager I tried to rewrite all the rules, staying up till the early hours, drinking, driving fast, eating rubbish, only to find out later in life that getting good sleep, only having one beer now and again (hey I'm not perfect), driving carefully and eating healthily is what actually improves the quality of my life. Getting back to my son, his "why" was less clear and convincing and he wasn't using what he'd learned. From the childish desire to play with friends and a selfless, carefree approach to language learning, he was now approaching Japanese fully aware of the daunting task ahead of him and letting it overwhelm him rather than enjoying the experience.

'What if I could show you a fun way to learn the numbers so you'll never forget them again?' I asked him.

I detected a raised eyebrow under his beanie which quickly turned into a suspicious gaze, but eventually he challenged with a defiant 'go on then!'

That is the right mindset to have under these circumstances: suspicious but open-minded. I was proud of him. The first step, I told him, was for me to know what the numbers are so we could come up with a plan.

Here they are :

1. ichi
2. ni
3. san
4. shi
5. go
6. roku
7. shichi
8. hachi
9. kyuu
10. yuu

So how would you go about getting these new words into your long term memory?

The trick is to make up a story about them. The more real, funny, bizarre the story is, the better. If you know anything about neuro-linguistic programming, or NLP, you will know to make the colours vivid, add in details to your story, hear noises, smell scents. I can't stress this enough: the more vivid and interesting you make your story, the more likely it is that your brain will want to retain it. This is actually how your brain works: not by memorising a list of words, but a sequence of images, a movie in your mind with related ideas or pictures. If your story involves being on a beach then MAKE IT REAL! Feel the sand; envisage the breeze blowing through your hair; hear the chatter of other people there, maybe seagulls are flying around; a slight drop in temperature as a cloud passes over and then a pleasing blast of heat as the sun comes out the other side, warming your back.

Make it as real and detailed as possible, like a HD film in your head with added scent and touch, and your memory will love you for it!

So what did I come up with to stick these numbers firmly into my son's mind?

I went through the words several times, not trying to think, just waiting for things to happen naturally. Now remember my son and I are both already polyglots so we had lots of words we could link to and my solution involved both Spanish and English. As I see it, this as just more justification for learning other languages and testament to the fact that learning one new foreign language makes further language learning much easier.

'Ichi, ni, san, shi, go' - was ridiculously easy to start with if you know English and a bit of Spanish.

Let me rewrite the words so you can see my thought process better:

Ichi ni san shi go

Itchy knee san, she go

To get to this you really only need to speak English. We all know what an itchy knee feels like. San, meanwhile, is Spanish for 'saint' and a male saint at that - a female saint would be "Santa" like Santa Barbara or Santa Ana in the US as opposed to a male saint like San Jose or San Francisco. Anyway, my purpose here was to create a mnemonic for my son to remember 1-10 in Japanese, not to be grammatically correct in Spanish. 'She go?' Ok, it's broken

English but it also fits with the bad grammar of 'San' being a female for my mnemonic and the overall image that is conjured (there's an example of the passive voice - notice I don't confirm who is doing the conjuring) with the goal of creating a mini-movie that I could embellish and re-run in my mind's eye.

In my head I saw an old woman, bent over and dressed in some kind of religious attire, maybe a habit, walking along but staggering as she scratched at the annoying itch on her knee. For some reason my mind leapt to the conclusion that she was crossing a river, and as water swashed over her calves, she held her habit up with one hand while the fingers on her other hand frantically scratched at the itch on her knee.

Ichi ni san shi go

Itchy knee san, she go

One two three four five

Watch the images, add detail, add sounds, feel the water, imagine your knee itching as you hold up your habit and try to alleviate the torment as the waters tug at your legs and threaten to pull you down. The water is cold, the fabric of your habit is coarse and you're in a rush. Is there any wind? What is the terrain like? What is the purpose of your journey? Where are you going and what will you do when you get there? What is the temperature? Can you see any wildlife nearby? Birds, cats, insects? Add all the details in. Really! If you can turn this into a 5D movie in your brain rather than a 2D badly drawn sketch you will up your success rate thousands of times over. This is powerful stuff. If you're reading this thinking it's rubbish, stop yourself, write yourself a list of ten random words and try it. Or even better, ask a friend or relative to suggest a list of ten random words so you know you're not cheating, use your imagination, find a way to link the new words to something similar, and then create your film. If you add the detail and colours, feelings, etc., you will find you can remember the list of words easily. The way to then get them into your long term memory, is to simply play the movie through in your mind's eye and then repeat the words as the movie prompts them. Imagine them in speech bubbles as the movie plays through. Do it often and do it repeatedly.

So at this point, we had 1-5. We were halfway through. 6-10 was a bit more random but with a little bit of imagination, and some less than perfect word choices, we got there.

- 6 roku
- 7 shichi
- 8 hachi
- 9 kyuu
- 10 yuu

My wife's cousin had a beautiful Yorkshire Terrier called Roco. I have no idea why, or where that name came from, but it's something I could link to and use, so I did.

Shichi sounds a lot like chichi in Spanish which is a euphemism for a lady's private parts. It's not a word I'd usually use in polite conversation, but it would probably amuse my son (him being fluent in Spanish and a teenager) which was a good enough reason for me! Then it was time for 'Hachi', 'kyuu' and 'yuu'. I'll be honest: I was a bit clueless as to how I was going to work them in, but I decided 'shichi' to 'hachi' was fairly simple, it at least rhymed - and 'kyu', yuu' (queue, you) could just be learned as normal words if needed. Having to actually work to memorise the last three numbers wasn't an issue for me when providing my son with a way to think about language and learning vocabulary that would help him for life. Putting a bit of work in was the least he could do.

So where are we with my movie? My itchy kneed saint was hobbling across the river, habit lifted in one hand, the other scratching at her knee, all the while carrying my wife's cousin's Yorkshire terrier "Roco" on her back and getting another itch in her most intimate female parts! These dratted habits were most definitely designed by men!

If you needed to *queue* to get *you* a silk one, you definitely would!

Itchy knee san, she go, roco (the yorkshire terrier) shichi (feminine bits) hachi (rhymes?) queue, you.

Ichi ni san shi go roku shichi hachi kyu yuu

1 2 3 4 5 6 7 8 9 10

Easy money! This whole process, by the way, probably took around 30 seconds. If you find yourself struggling to come up with something, it's just a matter of practising or asking someone what a word makes them think of. You'll soon get into the habit (excuse the pun). The trick is to make the frames of the movie flow, add detail, texture, feelings, sounds, and really experience the whole scenario you are making up. Make it distinctive, weird, funny if you can. In my story I can hear the water gurgling in the river, feel the cold of the water, a breeze ruffling my hair; I'm aware of my clothing and see the saint's halo and detail of the cross necklace hanging around her neck. You can perhaps add the words you are learning as subtitles that flash up as the scene progresses. The scene doesn't need fact-checking for the laws of physics or continuity - its only purpose is to help you remember. All of this will prompt your brain to prioritise building neurons to your long-term memory. Once you have your movie down pat, play it back to yourself several times a day. Repeat back the key words you are trying to learn. You don't generally need to switch between the movie and actually memorising the words, as if you make it vivid enough you will find that the movie eventually fades away to some extent while the vocab remains recorded in your long-term memory and your recall is quick. At the age of 45, I can still remember obscure words that I learnt when I was 17, and even if I may not have used a word since then, I can still pull it back to mind when needed.

Of course if you want to turn this newly memorised vocab into actual language, YOU NEED TO START USING IT! Again, you can't con your brain. Mnemonics are useful for getting large chunks of information into your head but won't make you fluent in a language on their own. While they will provide you with a big resource of words and tools to help you communicate, it is the communicating itself that builds fluency. Or to give you a clearer idea, think about it like this: having a lot of ingredients at your disposal doesn't make you a good cook. Stocking your kitchen with the best ingredients and tools, like knives, colanders, baking trays, measuring jugs, etc., means you have a lot of freedom with regards to what you can make. It also means making that meal is easier than if you had just your hands. But you only get good at cooking by cooking a lot!

SRS (SPACED REPETITION SOFTWARE) FLASHCARDS AND WHAT TO DO WITH THEM.

*W*hen approaching language learning with SRS, flashcards are usually used to show you an image and a word or a word in one language and its translation repeatedly. The repetition of each particular match changes in frequency as you learn but as the program suspects you are at risk of forgetting a particular match it will push it in front of you again to stop it slipping from your memory. As these systems become more intelligent they become more effective at helping you remember and recall vocabulary and scripts. This system has been much overhyped over the years and, in my estimation, has become an end unto itself and a major new industry with countless apps being created: Anki, Quizlet and Tinycards to name just a few.

Using spaced repetition for language learning was first suggested by C.A.Mace in 1932 so it's not a new system by any means but with the advent of the internet (and smartphones and apps in particular) if you're trying to learn a language it will be difficult to not come across these kinds of tools at some point. Should you use them? I would say definitely give them a try. However, there are a few observations I would make. The first thing that springs to mind is that when you match one word to another in the target language, you lose quite a bit of context. What you may think of as a house in the US or UK will differ quite a bit depending on which of those two countries you reside in. What this means is that, although you may have memorised a particular new word, the mapping of it isn't necessarily just going to work in all situations. Potentially, that word has other meanings that could be perceived in certain situations before the one you intended. This is why using a dictionary to look through several defini- tions of a word is helpful, as is hearing or reading it in context.

If you ask a Spanish person and a Chinese person to draw a picture of a 'meal' the results will likely be drastically different. Some words such as 'refuse' could have several meanings, such as to refuse an invitation. We could be talking about refuse as in rubbish/garbage. Or you could re-fuse an electrical system. That becomes difficult to map well with SRS and you'd have to have a different card for each meaning. Similarly, if you're learning a language with a different writing system - Japanese springs to mind where you have kanji and katakana - it becomes very complex to get all the relevant info onto the cards.

Another major concern is the cards themselves. Predominantly, one of two things can happen. Either you design your cards yourself - not ideal as you may initially make mistakes, have bad translations, etc., and use a very effective learning technique to cement those mistakes into your memory - or you could also end up spending time endlessly creating flashcards with amazing imagery for every piece of vocabulary in the language and not spend much time doing countless other tasks that would be far more valuable. If you're easily distracted, this would be a great way to waste hours of your day. The other thing you can do is use the cards provided by the app. This method doesn't make you immune to mistakes either though. Moreover, it's also not tailored for you personally and hence will be a little less effective.

At the end of the day though, what you are essentially doing is handing over the skill of working out your own mnemonics and giving it to a third party to do it for you. This is not a good idea. Finding memory techniques that work for you with the vocab you need to learn is one of the most important skills you will need as a polyglot. Once you practise it and flex that part of your brain you will start to automatically do it every time you look at a new word. The particular technique you use in each case will likely be more effective for you as you came up with it. There is no substitute for you doing it yourself and again, your brain will not be cheated. The other drawback to these apps is that, as I said in the previous chapter, language learning is not 100% vocab acquisition. It's about being able to communicate. If you're only using SRS apps to learn a language, you will never get there. You may have hundreds of words you can reel off as a list, but that's not the same as building a coherent and grammatically correct sentence that will be understood in another language. Again, having every ingredient under the sun doesn't make you a better cook. If you want to be a good cook, you need to cook a lot!

SRS apps can be used successfully for language learning when they comprise 5-10% of your overall language learning strategy. You can be totally successful in learning a language without them. If you're ONLY using them, I'd say you have close to 100% chance of failing. There is no magic wand for language learning. If you want to get fluent quickly you need to concentrate on being in conversation in that language to begin with, as well as listening and reading it too.

WHY LEARNING A LANGUAGE IS ACTUALLY FUN. (SOMETIMES RIB-CRACKINGLY HYSTERICAL!)

*W*e've discussed a bit about mindset already. If you want to learn a language and get fluent, mindset is paramount. You just have to know you will get fluent and enjoy the process. 'But I don't think I will ever be fluent, that's the issue', I hear you think. Think of something that you have got good at. There must be several things you can do well that you never thought you would become proficient at. Riding a bike? Cooking? Knitting? Golf? I can safely guess that whatever it is you're good at, you didn't start good. You were probably pretty awful at it initially but you carried on anyway through all the pain, frustration and headaches. Why? The answer is: you had the right mindset. You knew your "why" (albeit unconsciously). The key to learning anything is recreating that same mindset consciously, it's something you create, rather than something that happens to you.

You know you will become fluent, because you will work on it a little every day, with no thought of any time frame in mind. You will also commit to making mistakes and enjoying them when they happen - that means no embarrassment, humiliation or anger when you use a wrong word or someone points out a grammatical mistake. Imagine yourself making an error in English -'I would of done it' springs to mind as a common mistake in the UK, in place of the correct 'I would *have* done it' - and someone pointing out your mistake. The correct reaction is to immediately thank them and find the fun in why your brain made this error. Practice running over this scenario in your mind and feeling amused by it. Then when it actually happens in real life (and it will!) you will just laugh, maybe internally, and thank them. It won't be a negative experience, and you're rewarding the person that helped you stop making that mistake so they will be happy to help you further.

If you're prepared to risk everything to try and speak with only a 50% guess at the word you're trying to say, you will make some hilarious mistakes and mirth will often ensue.

We already mentioned my Spanish friend's elation with the English winter. Here are some of the mistakes I've made along my own journey.

I once walked into a Spanish supermarket wanting to buy some jam. At the time I was concerned with random chemicals being added into foods, E's and emulsifiers and food colourings etc. I had a look along the shelf, picked up a jar of jam: E300, ascorbic acid, I hadn't a clue what it meant, but surely it can't be good for you? I went to the counter and asked the cashier 'Do you have any jam that doesn't have preservatives in it?' In Spanish, what I actually said was 'Se vende mermelada sin preservativos?' Surprisingly the cashier was more health-conscious than I. She was a fanatic! 'Preservatives in the jam? Of course we don't put preservatives in the jam. That would be disgusting!', she practically spat at me whilst glowering disdainfully. I got the distinct impression I'd made some kind of error in my translation at this point but I couldn't work out what it was. When I got back home, I sat down to munch on my strawberry jam on toast and pore over my English to Spanish dictionary to try and work out where I'd gone wrong. I looked up jam.. *mermelada*, no issues there. I looked up to sell.. *vender* that all seemed good. I shuffled through the pages to P and traced my finger down till I came across preservatives... *conservantes*. Hmm, I wonder? I'd made a guess the word would be the same and came up with preservativos but it seems it's not used. Obviously, she'd recognised the word as she hadn't looked confused or stated she didn't understand me so it must exist in Spanish.

I flipped the dictionary to the back half, Spanish to English and again went to the letter P and traced down the page till I found preservativos... **condoms**. I think I sniggered at this point. I'd walked up to the cashier totally confidently and enquired as to whether they put condoms in their jam or not. I still laugh now when I remember her face. Of course, as my mindset was good, I proceeded to tell everyone I met about it. I told the Spanish class the next day what had happened and explained to the Spanish teacher what it meant in English and the whole class was laughing. Now I'll admit, my mindset at this stage wasn't consciously created, it had just happened that way so I can't claim credit here, things had just come together to make me very enthusiastic about Spanish but I did recreate it consciously later when I started to learn Italian (more about that later). This is a great example of finding fun in your mistakes: I didn't feel mortified, or even embarrassed about what happened in that supermarket. In fact, every time I thought about it I laughed. Mindset!

Another one that springs to mind happened in Italy. I was just picking up Italian and quite often if I didn't know the word, I had a 50/50 chance of getting it right by either "italifying" the English word or simply using the Spanish one.

For example, if I want to say 'forest' in Italian, I could use 'forest' from English or *bosque* from Spanish. If I used the English word I'd get it correct. 'Forest' in Italian is *foresta*, which is where we get the word from in English in the first place, either handed directly from Latin, or via old French. (I'd guess in this case from Latin as the French forêt has dropped an s̲).

'House' in Spanish is *casa*. If I went with the Spanish to guess my Italian translation, I'd get *la casa* in Italian and this would also be correct. This system gets you to the right translation a huge percentage of the time. However, when it goes wrong, it can go very wrong.

I'd been in Italy for about a week and a half and had started speaking at a conversational level within a week. I used a mix of approaches to learn this quickly, which we'll cover later, however, a LOT of guesswork was involved. My hair was getting a bit long on top - not a problem I'd have to deal with too much in later life unfortunately - so I decided to have it cut. Italian was my fifth language (if we include English) so confidence was not an issue. I could think with a very small set of words and have a good guess at other words I needed or explain my way around them on the fly.

I jumped on the bus into town and strolled into the hairdressers with a swagger. 'I'd like to have my hair cut please!', I announced to the surprise of the girl at the counter. In formulating this sentence I'd relied a bit too heavily on my fluent Spanish. It dawned on me as I walked through the door and started working out what I wanted to say that I didn't know the Italian word for 'hair'. I knew from German that hair is a Germanic word (Haar) so my best option was to use the Spanish word *pelo*. 'Vorrei tagliarmi i peli per piacere,' - is what I came out with in Italian.

This wasn't the only other mistake I'd made either before or since the jam/condom fiasco in Spain. It's something you deal with regularly if you learn languages. I'd passed through this situation thousands of times over the years and so I could recognise instantly that her puzzled expression didn't quite fit the seemingly day-to-day request of asking for a haircut at the hairdresser's. I wasn't quite sure just where I'd gone wrong... A quirk of grammar can sometimes throw the meaning of a sentence way off, but a good guess was that *pelo* in Spanish didn't quite have the same connotation as *pelo* in Italian. Again, if the word didn't exist, she more likely would have said: 'cut what?' So I guessed it existed but wasn't quite the right word. Never mind, I'm a language pro, not a big problem for me, I pointed at my head and repeated 'I want to cut these.' *Ah certo, i capelli!* She informed me (of course, your hair!) Great, now I had learned the right word so I thanked her for correcting me. If I'd thought of the other Spanish word for hair *el cabello,* I would have guessed correctly and said *capelli* (which is plural, and the singular would be *capello* {*cabello*} which is only one letter of difference really), but where would the fun be in that?

I got back home with my new *coiffed* barnet and sat down at the table with my dictionary to look up what *peli* meant in Italian. It turns out it does mean 'hair', but not the hair on your head. It refers to body hair, possibly facial hair and of course pubic hair. It's not always easy to get a sense of how something comes across to a native speaker by looking at dictionary definitions so I ran what I said by a few of my Italian friends to try and understand what images it would conjure up in their minds. Seemingly the fact that I'd coupled *peli* with the word 'cut', rather than shave, meant I'd eliminated the conclusion that I was referring to facial or body hair. I didn't have a beard and both facial hair and most body hair would be shaved, leaving the only conclusion that I was looking to have my pubic hair trimmed! I've come across a few forums of Italians discussing the difference between *peli* and *capelli* and they seem genuinely surprised that English only has the one word for both. 'They are so different!'- someone had written on one message board. It's interesting trying to get into the other language at this deep level and being able to see how they can think about things in subtly different ways because of grammar or difference in terminology and culture.

Re-analysing the word now, it makes more sense. We can break the word down like this: *capelli* is the plural so one would be *capello*; we can further break down *capello* as 'cap' and 'pello', which brings us back to 'pelo'. So what does 'cap' mean? The short answer is that it means "head" although it's not the word used in modern Italian. In Italy you will normally hear one's head referred to as *la testa*. For example, the famous Lamborghini *Testarossa* literally means 'redhead'. But you will hear 'il capo' used to describe the head of a division or team (seemingly synonymous with "boss") and also as in "headland" so Cape Town in South Africa would be Città del Capo. The Spanish word *cabo* is also used in the geographical context, whereas one's anatomical head is *cabeza*. It's interesting to note that 'p' changes to a 'b' in Spanish turning *capo* into *cabo* and *capello* into *cabello*. There are lots of examples of this you will pick up when you learn languages where sounds drift a bit, like the example earlier where 'forest' in french becomes *forêt*, dropping an 's', which is a common feature of French. Other examples are hôpital (hospital) and *île* (isle). It seems the little hat over the letter in each French word here appears to actually signify that the 's' has been dropped rather than changing the pronunciation or stress - fascinating! These words were incorporated into English from Norman French and so the 's' was probably dropped from modern French sometime after the 11th Century.

So literally *peli* in Italian is 'hair' and *capelli* is 'head hair'. The interesting thing here is it seems it's actually English that is the odd language out. Most languages have one word for head hair and another for body hair. It seems English also did at one time but it was dropped at some point. So the fact some Italians ponder why English doesn't have two different words would suggest they don't consciously analyse the word *capelli* as a compound noun of *capo* and *pelli* but as a singular word in its own right.

HOW TO BECOME AWARE OF
YOUR LANGUAGE.

*M*any years later I found myself working in a call centre in Belgium. I was employed to handle international calls using English, Spanish, German and Italian, the languages I had written on my c.v. My fifth language was French and was also the first foreign language I'd studied. I had done the A-level at college but, though I could get by in France, it wasn't business level, having never lived there.

Before arriving in Belgium, I'd been living in Spain for the ten years prior and hadn't used much Italian for that entire decade as I was now in my thirties and in a settled relationship, and travel had dropped to a minimum due to financial constraints. We arrived in Belgium from Spain as a result of the

Credit Crunch of 2009 and went to Germany and France quite a lot as Belgium is a very small country. Germany was two hours away, France about two hours' drive as well; a 40 minute drive would bring you to the border of the Netherlands where they speak Dutch; Luxembourg was also nearby, where a mix of French and German was spoken, at about three hours' drive. This meant my Italian alone wasn't really being used and the fact that I was also learning Dutch, didn't leave me much time to do anything about it. I was a bit concerned about how I'd get on as I had already struggled a bit with my English. The reason for that was just coincidental. Two other people had started the job at the same time as me and they trained the three of us together.

The other two (a man and a woman both from Brazil) spoke fluent Portuguese of course, but also English and Spanish. Our trainer was from Colombia and spoke Spanish and French with good English but she wasn't as confident in it as she was in Spanish and French. We had a quick exchange and the consensus was it was easier for everyone to do the training in Spanish, so that's what happened. Four weeks passed and we were let loose on the telephones. As we had trained in Spanish the phone system was initially set to only let Spanish calls come through to us until we gained confidence in the job. However, only a few days later my system was updated to accept English calls as well. A call came in and I needed to explain what the situation was in my mother tongue. The job involved troubleshooting and resolving problems so I worked back through my training, thinking in Spanish as that is how we'd been trained, made sure I'd come to the right conclusion and suddenly realised I didn't know what the word was in English that we'd been using on a daily basis in training. I knew the word in Spanish and its meaning was obvious but when I tried to put it into English it sounded wrong and the meaning wasn't clear at all. It's one thing to guess or explain your way around things when you're learning a language but this was a professional setting. I'd been employed as a fluent speaker of multiple languages and here I was struggling to form a sentence in my mother tongue. I coughed and apologised to the customer and asked if they wouldn't mind holding the line for a few minutes while I did some checks. He obliged and I stuck him on mute while I turned to the colleague sitting next to me and in a panic asked him what the translation was in English. He looked at me a bit bewildered, 'But you're English!', he advised me. I did a quick check… Yup, I think he's right! 'I know', I told him, 'But I've never talked about this before in English so I don't know the words!'

Later on, I was advised that German and Italian were to be added to my incoming call rota. I prepared and looked up all the vocab that I was already using in Spanish and English and made sure I knew bulk translations for the most regular phrases being used in the job. I was a bit hesitant about working with Italian. I'd studied German and Spanish to degree level, but I'd never studied Italian formally. I'd picked it up more like a child would and by using my knowledge of all my other languages as a springboard. My first call was a bit awkward, but as soon as I started speaking it felt like getting back on a bike, words suddenly popped up in my brain that I hadn't used for ten years or more and the sentences started to flow. By the end of the first week of using Italian again, I was as comfortable as I was using English or Spanish.

Why have I told you this story? It highlights some salient points. Firstly, you never stop learning a language, even if you only learn one, your mother tongue. If you read a technical manual, or a very good novel I'm sure words crop up now and again in

English that you've not seen before and you have to ask or look them up (or you just skip over them). So, you shouldn't feel bad when it happens in another language. If you listen to experts discussing maths or chemistry or things like computer coding you can quickly get lost in the jargon they use and feel like they're talking another language. The same happened to me in that call centre. I struggled in English because I didn't prepare for what I would be discussing, assuming my English, being native, was impeccable, and it wasn't. Secondly, to hold a conversation on one topic you need a surprisingly small set of vocabulary. I was extremely worried about my Italian, but as I had thoroughly prepared, and essentially at work we discussed the same issues over and over again using the same vocabulary and set phrases, it was extremely quick and easy to get into the flow of it.

What does this mean for you? Become aware of what you want to talk about. What do you want to use the language for? If you want to read *manga* comics in Japanese, it's advisable to start there and not learn how to order a sandwich. You will of course at some point need to learn all of it, but start with what you're actually interested in first as that keeps your motivation to learn at its highest. If you want to learn French because it sounds lovely, take note of what you talk about in English. What topics do you discuss at work? What vocabulary are you using? What sentences are repeated over and over? If you deal with customers face to face or over the phone you probably trot out some kind of welcome without giving it much thought: *Hello welcome to xxx, how can I help?* What do you chat about with your partner or friends and family? What are your hobbies? Go and look up vocabulary around those topics and jot down obvious sentences that are related. I found I could chat all day in Italian at work when it came to things related to my job. But suddenly, when I went for a lunch break with an Italian colleague, general chit-chat surprisingly became a struggle as I wasn't using that kind of general vocabulary on a day-to-day basis. My conversation was only fluent whilst centred around my job. Eventually, this improved with time but the point is still valid. Make your life easier, keep the interest and motivation up and make sure you're learning the language the way you'd actually speak your mother tongue. Become aware of your language!

HOW I LEARNED ITALIAN IN ONE WEEK!

*Y*es, I really did. I wasn't speaking perfect Italian in one week. But 7 days after arriving I was able to sit down at a table for a meal with an Italian family and participate in the conversation. This is a lot easier than you might think and I achieved it with a combination of everything we have discussed so far, along with a few other bits and pieces I may not have mentioned.

First of all, I worked out a plan to be able to converse within seven days. I could skip a lot of the steps most people would need as I'd already learned other languages and through learning them garnered a deep understanding of languages in general, how they are structured and how that relates to English. I knew I needed to be able to conjugate verbs, and know how to order words in a sentence to express who did what to whom. I needed to handle speaking in different tenses to communicate when things were happening: today, yesterday, last year, next week, etc. I needed to check if there was a case system or a subjunctive and what the rules for them were. I understood I may need to agree adjectives and deal with masculine, feminine and possibly neuter nouns. I was prepared for the fact there may be things I'd come across in Italian that I hadn't encountered in other languages and rather than have that be daunting I was excited to expand on my knowledge of how languages worked. I knew I'd have to come up with mnemonics to help get new vocab into my long-term memory and that I'd already have a good grasp of a lot of words from the mix of English, Spanish and French I had in my head already. Most importantly, there was no doubt in my mind that I could achieve my goal. The doubt was in how perfectly I'd speak. But my aim wasn't perfection, it was simply communication and I knew that was within my reach - of this I was 100% confident.

DAY 1.

I sat down and wrote a list of all the words that I would need to have a basic conversation (bearing in mind the setting and the people I would be speaking to). I was staying with an Italian host family. The father was a businessman, the wife a psychologist and the two children were students. I started with really basic stuff:

Knife, fork, plate, salt, cup, table, chair, orange juice, water, etc.

I also looked up the basic adjectives I would need: big, small, old, young, hot, cold, wet, dry, up, down, names of colours, numbers up to 20, etc, etc.

Next, I looked up Italian word order and found that, like Spanish and French, they generally put the adjective after the noun, not before as we'd do in English.

So where we would say 'the big car', they say 'the car big'.

Next, adjectives agree in gender and number.

We say 'the big cars' (the 's' telling us there is more than one car)

They say 'the cars bigs' (so if English worked the same way, when adding an 's' to 'car' to make it plural, you would also have to add one to the adjective).

Going back to what we discussed in previous chapters, I'd regularly think like this in English to assist in translating and to help my brain adapt to the mental gymnastics required to think "out of order" like this. So, I'd think 'I want some new shoes' and then rethink, 'I want some shoes news'. I found it easier to make funny sounding sentences in English. Do it often enough and it starts to become normal and then to doing it in Spanish or Italian is just a small further step to take. I didn't need to do this in Italian as I could jump straight to thinking in Italian, which initially is probably the hardest thing to do learning a language unless you have got to that level at least once before in a foreign language (in which case you can do it pretty much instantly in my experience). Still, if you're on your first language, I'd recommend it as a good stepping stone exercise.

I looked up if Italian had feminine and masculine nouns. It did, and also (surprisingly to me) neuter, which I'd come across in German but had not seen in a Romance language before. With this knowledge

I learned how to make plurals from singular nouns. In Italian, '1 pizza' becomes '2 pizze', which differs from the '1 pizza'/ '2 pizzas' pattern we see in English or Spanish, while masculine nouns are pluralized like this: *il gatto* (the cat) *i gatti* (the cats).

I found there were a lot of irregular features in Italian, things that didn't follow set patterns, but I didn't trouble myself with learning them. While getting them wrong would make me look stupid it wouldn't stop me from being understood. My aim was to communicate, not get bogged down in detail, and I figured I would pick them up on the fly as I got corrected in natural conversation - as long as I kept thanking people for correcting me, they'd keep correcting me and I'd keep learning. This is an important point. The tipping point in language learning is when you get to the chatting stage. The quicker you can get there the better, so anything that is extraneous to that aim, in my opinion, is a waste of time. I didn't faff around learning the several different ways to make plurals in Italian. For example, in English, the plural of 'mouse' is not 'mouses', but 'mice'. This is the kind of mistake a foreigner is very likely to make, but you will still understand him. Let every task you undertake get you one step closer to getting to the chatting stage. Worry about perfecting after that, and things will be MUCH easier for you in the long run. This obviously doesn't mean you won't have to learn all the other stuff. I'm just saying don't focus on it at the beginning.

Once I had my lists and translations, I quickly made up some mnemonics for them (with constant practice, this can be done instinctively upon first glancing at a new word). In reality, I was doing this as I was looking the words up in the dictionary for the most part.

DAY 2.

Now it was time for verbs and prepositions. Again, I sat down and looked up a list of the most basic verbs I would need.

To be, to have, to want, to see, to ask, to call, to pass, to eat, to drink, etc.

Next, I looked up the conjugations. It was very similar to Spanish which made my job much easier. I looked up if there was a formal versus informal conjugation - there was - and then I looked up basic prepositions (e.g. in, of, over, under, from, to, by, etc.)

I looked up the basics of asking questions: how, what, why, when, who, where, etc. I then started making up sentences:

The salt is on the table.

The orange juice is by the salt.

Please pass the salt.

Where are the forks?

Who is your friend?

I had an Italian friend check them to make sure I wasn't making up gibberish and noted any mistakes I had made and adjusted my thinking to take them into account.

DAY 3.

Tenses. The basic tenses are present, past and future but I knew from my other language studies that some languages had more than one past tense. Spanish for example has four compared to English's three. There was also the subjunctive which English doesn't have (for the most part) and specific ways of making the future tense in Romance languages that aren't used in Germanic languages like English and

German so I had a good idea of what I was likely to find. All I had to do was find out the specific rules in Italian and plug them into my existing knowledge base of languages.

I again made up some sentences...

The salt was on the table. Now it is not.

The orange juice will be in the fridge if it is not on the table by the salt.

Who did you talk to yesterday?

What have you done with the forks?

DAYS 4 & 5.

I went to the bookshop and bought myself a novel by one of my favourite authors written in Italian - *specifically one I hadn't* read before. This is really important to start with. The temptation is to get one you have read already to make it easier, but then you start guessing at the sentences and trying to remember what was happening rather than looking things up and it's actually counterproductive. If you love the author and haven't read the book before, your motivation is at its highest to really get into the story. If you've already read it, it's easy to tell your-

self it's ok to stop, you already know what happens
in the book. Never mind, you think, this isn't for me.
Bad move! The other thing I've seen people do is to
get two copies of the book, one in English and one
in the target language. Then if they get stuck, they
can check what it says in English, this will, they
correctly think, save them the time flicking through
the dictionary, the translation is already there for
them. This is also a big mistake. Making yourself
look the word up in the dictionary and then writing
it down as far as your brain is concerned is using the
vocabulary so it's more likely to store it in your
long-term memory. If you're just flicking your eyes
to the other book and seeing what the English is on
the other page, it's the short-term memory bank for
you every time! Ultimately you end up reading
further and further down the page in English, skim-
reading the words in the foreign language book until
eventually you find you're halfway through the
English book and the foreign book is still on page 1!
It's a complete waste of time.

Going back to the book, on the first page I had to
look up pretty much every single word. Once I had
them all I started re-reading from the top of the page
and trying to work out the meaning of the sentences.
If I got to a word and I couldn't remember what it

meant, rather than checking my list, I'd look it up in the dictionary and write the English and Italian next to each other again in different colours. I could easily forget the same word four or five times in two pages and have to look them up and write them down each time, but if words are cropping up that often they're obviously VERY important in the language and therefore worth remembering!

Pages 1 and 2 were painful. On page 3 I looked up 90% of the words on the page.

By page 10, I was only looking up about 50% of the words. By the end of the first chapter, I was looking up maybe 10-20% of the words on each page. By the time I'd got halfway through the book I'd only have to look up one or two words tops on each page and some pages I could read without looking up a single word.

It's worth clarifying here my list-writing method. When I started on page 1 I jotted down every single word I didn't know: English on the left in blue ink; Italian on the right in green ink. This is called anchoring. You anchor the Italian word to the English word in your memory this way. Use bright colours to help your mind remember. I've seen people say this is a bad idea, as you want the target language to be learned more like a child would - which is a fair point - but let me tell you a story about when I studied languages with many bilingual kids during college. It just so happened there was a Spanish lad who'd moved to the UK when he was little and was fluent in English, an Italian boy who had an Italian father and English mother and a girl who had a German father and English mother. All three of them perfectly bilingual. However when it came to translating they struggled as much as the rest of us with anything but rudimentary sentences. They of course had the added advantage that their vocabulary was immense, but they sometimes struggled to cross over simple words from one language to the other. Why? Because they were bilingual, they'd learned both languages to native level *independently*. They didn't have their vocabulary anchored. I'm not saying they couldn't easily learn to do this, of course, they could, but in my opinion it's easier to do as you go along. And while you're trying to get over the initial translating-in-your-head phase that you will pass through at least with your first foreign language, it will help you. I meticulously wrote down a word each time I couldn't remember the meaning, even when I knew with certainty that I'd already looked it up several times before. I always jotted down the English and then the Italian and did them in different colours. This anchors the Italian word to the English word in your mind. Remember this is how your brain works: bright vivid images. The point was NOT to ever go back and read the lists and memorise them. I have pages and pages on multiple A4 pads of long lists of words in all sorts of languages and I have NEVER gone back and read them. So what's the point of writing them out? By looking them up and writing them down you ARE USING THEM and you might not realise it but your subconscious picks up on it and begins work on the long-term memory neural connections you will need to keep them available at all times. The colours aid your brain - pick strong, easy to read colours which contrast well against the page, and remember your brain processes information as images and the brighter and more vivid the easier it is to remember. It helps, where practical, to think of a motion image of whatever it is you are writing down as you do this for added impact on your memory. This system is pretty annoying when you *know* you've already looked up a particular word and it's just not going in. The trick here is to recognise that annoyance is going to focus your attention if you can be aware of it, that this is a word you need to concentrate more on. If you know you've written this word down several times before and you can't remember it still this means: 1) the word is important; 2) the word has high frequency; 3) you should make an extra effort to make it memorable. Maybe create a mnemonic for it as you write it down. The annoyance here is an alarm bell highlighting something useful. Recognise the prickling of that annoyance but don't let yourself get annoyed. Instead, use it as a tool to pick out blind spots in your learning process and be grateful for it as it can push you forward on your journey to fluency!

As a side note, in my humble opinion, this is a much better method than SRS flashcards. Yes, it's hard work (let's face, it SRS is practically passive learning in comparison), but reading hones so many skills at once: you're getting context, you're seeing sentence structure and gaining comprehension skills, taking in idiomatic language... There's no preparation of flashcards required or working out which words you want to translate, and you're getting the vocab you need with the correct frequency. The most common words are coming at you again and again. Just make sure you are writing down the words as prescribed - for me this is one of the best ways to acquire and retain vocab. Again, this won't make you fluent - you can only get fluent by speaking and listening - but vocab makes it easier to speak and understand. It's the colours you paint your picture with.

DAY 6.

I sat down at the table with my host family. Up to this point I'd used a mix of Spanish, English and French to communicate with them. But I hadn't attempted to speak any Italian. I'd done this on purpose. I wanted it to be dramatic, with the antici-pation of getting a very positive and surprised response that would hopefully counteract the terrible Italian I would be coming out with: gram-matical mistakes, incorrect word use, terrible accent, etc. I'm a realist: I knew I wasn't going to be speaking pretty in just six days, so I needed the fact that I just started chatting with them in Italian as if I'd been practising it for months to be a big enough of a surprise to them that the flaws in it wouldn't detract from my attempts. I also felt a fair bit of pressure as they knew I was a language student and already spoke several languages, so there was some degree of expectation that I should be quite good at this.

We ate as they chatted away about this and that. I tried to follow the conversation as much as possible, then when I felt confident and knew where the conversation was going, I chipped in with my opinion. They had started talking about languages and how difficult they are to learn, which (given the number of languages that had been flying around that table over the last few days) was an obvious and constant topic.

'Io credo che solitamente sia molto difficile imparare altre lingue ma può essere anche facile se sai come farlo.' (I think it's usually very difficult to learn other languages but it can also be easy if you know how to do it.)

The mother nearly spat her farfalle out, the father blinked several times and then, mouth wide open, straight gawked at me. The two kids, who were roughly my age and knew I was studying but didn't know how far along I was (remember I'd only been in Italy with them for six days at this point), grinned at each other and at their parents' reaction.

I was fairly confident at this point that the reaction was genuine surprise at me suddenly coming out with what may have not been a perfectly grammatical and well-pronounced sentence, but perfectly understandable to them. Not only that, but their surprise wasn't due to the fact I'd made another faux pas along the jam/condom or peli/capelli lines. I'd made sure to stick only to words I knew and kept the sentences simple.

'Ryan, you speak Italian!' The mother proclaimed, 'I can't believe it! How did you do it in one week?' 'Bravo Ryan,' said the father. 'Grazie mille' ("thank you very much"), I told them, feeling rather pleased with myself. We continued the conversation in (for me broken) Italian and I didn't look back.

HOW TO MASTER GRAMMAR

So far in this book, we have already covered some of the basic elements of grammar: things like how to make plurals, word order, things like subject, verbs and objects, and active versus passive voice. In this section, I will try to cover and recap some of the most basic things you need to know, which tend to be assumed knowledge in a lot of the language books I've seen. The hope is this will help you on your way to learning your first foreign language. I'm going to explain the concepts in English using examples in English where possible, without you having to try and consider it via a foreign language, which will hopefully make things a thousand times easier for you. In some cases where the concept doesn't exist in English (or I can't think of a good example), I will use foreign language examples, which may pique your interest and arouse your curiosity in some other languages you may not be familiar with.

Please note, although I have a rudimentary knowledge of quite a few languages from around the globe, the languages I'm most knowledgeable about are all European ones. This is because, being English, I live in Europe and most of the countries I travel to are European and so these languages are the obvious choice for work and leisure for me. I mention this as if you are intending to learn Chinese or Arabic or a host of other languages I could name, there are going to be grammatical features I'm likely unaware of and hence they will not be covered here. Having said that, this guide is very basic, so will still cover most of what you need to know as an absolute beginner. Also bear in mind I'm not an English major - my knowledge of English grammar is entirely centred around learning foreign languages and the terms I will use will be those you find in language learning books. I don't profess to be an English grammar expert. I am however expert at mapping English grammar in the linguistic sense, to that of other languages.

With that said, here are the most basic and fundamental grammatical terms you should learn and
have an understanding of to help you on your
journey to learning a second language. Don't try to
memorise them per se. A general awareness that
they exist is a good enough start. You will come
across them again once you (re)commence learning a
language and hopefully, you will then have a famil-
iarity with the terms and their functions.

1. THE DEFINITE AND INDEFINITE ARTICLE.

The definite article is quite simply the word 'the' in
English as in 'the cat' or 'the dog'. The indefinite
article is the word 'a' as in 'a cat' or 'a dog'.

This is one of those little gems that, if you ask most
native speakers about, they won't be able to explain
what the difference is. Have a quick think and see if
you can figure out what the difference between 'a
cat' and 'the cat' is?

Did you get it?

The definite article refers to a subject that is known
or definite whereas the indefinite article refers to an
unknown or indefinite subject.

For example, 'The man saw a cat' we know which man we are talking about - the one that saw a cat - but we don't know which cat he saw specifically. It could have been any cat, we just know he saw one. It couldn't have been any *man* though. The man we are talking about is the man that saw a cat, not any other man.

Compare this to the sentence: 'A man saw the cat'. In this case, we know which cat we are talking about, but we're not sure which man saw it specifically.

If the subtle difference still isn't clear, think of it this way: imagine you have a child in front of you with a red plate and a blue plate. The child holds one coloured plate in each hand and raises their hands. They drop one of the two plates and it crashes to the floor. You are asked: 'What happened?'. You would answer 'the child dropped the plate'. '**The** child' as we know which child it was and '**the** plate' as we know which of the two plates was dropped, we saw it.

Compare that to a similar scenario: the child again raises two plates in their hands but this time you are blindfolded. Then you hear something crash to the floor and you are asked 'What happened?' Yet again. You could answer: 'the child dropped **a** plate'. The child is still known so we say '**the** child', but now it's not clear which plate was dropped so we say '**a** plate' (one of the two, but we're not sure which).

Quite often we'll switch from the indefinite to the definite to introduce and then refer back to a new subject in a sentence.

'There was **an** apple on the table. The man ate **the** apple'. In the first instance, we talk about **an** apple as it is a new subject; in the second instance we refer back to it as **the** apple, as we already know which apple we are referring to, (the one on the table). Some languages don't have this distinction at all. Japanese uses marker words to introduce a new subject in a sentence for example but there is no word for 'the' or 'a'.

A good tip for most European languages that, in addition to articles, also have gender (like German, French, Spanish, etc) is to always learn the article with the word. So in Spanish, don't learn that the word for 'house' is *casa*, learn that the word for 'house' is *la casa*. Especially in languages like German, it's much harder to know just by looking at a word what the gender is. Take for example 'the girl': you would expect it to take the feminine word for 'the' (*die*) but it doesn't - it takes the neuter: *das*.

So rather than learning the word for 'girl' as *Mädchen* learn and write down "**das** *Mädchen*. This will save you going back later on and having to relearn what gender all the words you know are. Similarly in Spanish, words ending with an <u>a</u> (as a general rule) are feminine. E.g. <u>la</u> play**a**, <u>la</u> tas**a**, <u>la</u> espad**a** all follow that rule, but <u>el</u> di**a** does not. Learning the exceptions can be off-putting as it *seems* difficult. I reframed this to myself as a standout point. If I made an effort to learn the irregulars, it would mark me up as a cut above other non-native speakers that usually made these kinds of mistakes, resulting in surprise and a native speaker being impressed with my knowledge of their language. It's definitely worth the extra couple of seconds to make a mental note as you learn the word.

2. NOUNS AND ADJECTIVES.

We have already briefly covered these. Nouns are names of people, things or places and adjectives describe them. Adjectives can go in front of or behind the noun depending on the rules of the specific language you are learning. Interestingly in French, the meaning of the adjective can sometimes change depending on its position.

Ma propre chambre – means 'my own room'

Ma chambre propre – means: 'my clean room'

So you could say in French ma *propre chambre propre* which would mean 'my own clean room'. Find out which goes first in your target language.

3. QUESTION WORDS AND HOW TO MAKE A QUESTION

When you start learning anything you're probably going to be asking a lot of questions. One of the most useful phrases to first learn when you're acquiring another language is 'how do you say....' while pointing at something or similarly 'what is that called?'

This means you're actively straight to the point of using the language and picking up the vocabulary you need on the fly. So learning how to ask questions is pretty important.

You will come across a few ways of constructing questions but there are three basic ones and these are: using interrogative's (question words), using inversions, or just simply using an upward inflection in your voice at the end of the sentence.

The basic question words you should learn are: 'how', 'why', 'what', 'who', 'when', 'where', 'which'. Most of these can even be used as sentence words (one word sentences), meaning you can ask a question without even forming a phrase. You can point at an empty train platform and ask 'when?' and point at your watch and most people are going to guess what you *want* to know.

'How much' or 'how many' in English is also extremely useful and some languages have just one word for this, for example the Italian 'quanto?'

The other method for making questions is just to invert or swap the subject and the verb.

'It **is** cold' - is a statement

'**Is** it cold?' – is a question.

You can of course in spoken language as mentioned before, just raise your voice up at the end of a sentence.

'The trains here are usually on time?'

The interesting thing with grammar is there are lots of solutions to expressing the same ideas. For example, some languages stick suffixes onto words to make them questions, which is also a really cool way to do it.

In the language spoken in Finland, they can add the suffix *-ko* or *-kö* to a word to make it a question.

Olen means 'I am'

Olenko would mean 'am I?'

4. PRONOUNS, VERBS AND ADVERBS

In most European languages there are six persons and, though not emphatically expressed the standard way of writing them down when conjugating a verb is fairly logical.

We can view them thus:

- 1st person singular / 1st person plural
- 2nd person singular / 2nd person plural
- 3rd person singular / 3rd person plural

What this actually refers to is the subject doing the verb.

The first person singular is 'I', as in 'I sang'

The second person singular is 'you', as in 'you sang'

The third person singular is 'he' or 'she' or 'it', as in 'he/she/it sang'

The plurals, if you think about it, refer to the singular pronoun plus another or others.

If I want to refer to myself ('I') and someone else doing something then I use the pronoun 'we'.

The first person plural is 'we', which refers to the fact that I do it and someone else does it too.

Now one of the quirks of English is that it lost one of its original pronouns in the 2nd person.

Originally in English, we would have had 'thou' for the singular and 'you' for the plural

So if you said 'thou art great' you would be talking to one person whereas 'you are great' would refer to several people. 'Thou' eventually dropped away and we now just have 'you'. We are obviously still aware there is a distinction in English as most English speaking countries have reinvented a slang informal plural form of 'you', which is a bit strange really as *'you'* was already originally the plural form and it was the singular that dropped away. This has now led to the form 'y'all' in the US and most of the rest of the English speaking world has 'you's' or 'ye's'.

The third person 'he/she/it' in the plural would be he, she or it and someone or something else giving us the pronoun 'they'.

If we map these using the verb 'to be' we can clearly see that you is in fact the plural as its conjugation matches the other plurals

- Singular (s) vs Plural (pl)
- 1st person (s) I am / 1st person (pl) we **are**
- 2nd person (s) thou art (now archaic) / 2nd person (pl) you **are**
- 3rd person (s) he/she/it is /3rd person (pl) they **are**

Note that all the plural form endings are '**are**'.

Adverbs are to verbs as adjectives are to nouns, i.e. they describe them.

So a rabbit may be quick

but it runs quickly.

'The quick rabbit' has a noun with an adjective in front.

'It runs quickly' has a verb and an adverb.

RYAN DOHERTY

Interestingly in English adjectives go before the noun but adverbs tend to go after the verb. Peculiar isn't it? We may at first struggle with having to put the adjective after the noun in Romance languages, but we do it with adverbs with no thought at all.

Many adverbs are built out of adjectives similar to 'quick/quickly', for example: 'the fierce man', fierce being the adjective. If you want to use this word to describe a verb instead of a noun you can just add the suffix '-ly' to get 'fiercely' as in 'the man fought fiercely'.

Little rules like this are handy to know and apply consciously because once you know it, any adjectives you learn can mostly then also be used as adverbs. For example, the suffix '-ly' to turn an adjective into an adverb in Spanish would be *-mente*.

The rule in Spanish is: you take an adjective like *rápido*, use the feminine form so it becomes *rápida* and add the suffix *-mente*

*El coche aceleró rapida**mente*** (the car accelerated rapidly). So, knowing this simple rule, you could see a sentence in Spanish such as *bailaba alegremente* and already infer a lot from it without even knowing Spanish or recognising either of the two words.

We can have a good guess that *alegremente* is an adverb as it ends in *-mente*. We can also infer that the English translation of it will likely end in '-ly 'and it does: *alegre* means 'happy; and *alegremente* would be 'happily'. Moreover, we can deduce that, as the second word *alegremente* is an adverb, the first word must be a verb!

This is really useful to know because when you go to look up *bailaba* in your dictionary you may not find it - the reason being it is a verb and it's been conjugated. The basic form (or what is referred to as the infinitive form) would be *bailar* and it means 'to dance'. To save space, many dictionaries will only list the infinitive form of each verb and they'll leave it up to you to work back the conjugation. If you thought *bailaba* was a noun you would now be lost but because you know it is a verb, you could - if you knew a few other basic grammar rules - actually work out what the infinitive of the verb would be.

You should now see how just knowing some very simple grammar rules is going to really reinforce your language acquisition, not only giving you some extra insight into what is happening to who, that you may have picked up subconsciously but can now infer consciously, but also helping you understand what function other words in the sentence may be serving and hence providing clues on likely meanings even if you don't recognise the words themselves.

5. VERB CONJUGATION

Verb conjugation is essentially when you take the infinitive form of a verb - which in English takes the form 'to something' (as in 'to think', 'to dance', 'to eat') - and manipulating that word to convey further meaning about who, when and if!!

Learning verb conjugations is one of those things many dread. Writing down lists of verb conjugations and trying to commit them to memory is no one's idea of fun - that's why I don't do it. Most languages will follow some kind of pattern in their verb conjugation. There are always the irregular forms, but if you initially learn the basic patterns in the present tense, you will very quickly get to the talking stage, which we've discussed, is where you want to be to get fluent as quickly as possible.

Getting a verb conjugation wrong will generally not stop a native speaker from understanding you, but not conjugating at all will lead to very stilted and difficult to understand speech.

Verb conjugation in English is pretty straightforward for the most part but we'll use the verb 'to be' which should throw up quite a few irregularities and give you the mindset to learn a foreign language.

Here is the conjugation of the verb 'to be' in the present tense.

- I am / We are
- You are
- He/she/it is / They are

We can note that the singular form of the verb 'to be' changes for every person, i.e. We don't say 'I be', 'you be', 'it be', etc. The verb 'to be' completely changes beyond recognition in the first person to become 'I am'. Similarly, 'he/she/it is' doesn't seem to bear much resemblance to the original infinitive 'to be' nor does it to 'am'. *'You are',* as previously discussed is actually the old plural form - the singular *'thou'* was lost in the annals of history. At least with the plurals 'we are', 'you are' and 'they are' there is some consistency but again the form 'are' doesn't seem to have much to do with the infinitive 'to be'. This is because *'to be'* and its conjugations are a motley crew of roots that have come from various different languages and clotted together mysteriously to become the bane of foreign students learning English. If we add in the past tense versions 'were/was' it gets even more convoluted. There seems to be no rhyme or reason to how these words originated from the original verb 'to be' and that's because they didn't originate from it at all. They've actually been amalgamated into it.

Normally you could take a conjugation in English, for example *'I dance'*, and work out that the infinitive is *'to dance'*, or *'he sings'* the infinitive is *'to sing'*. But what do we make of the following conjugations 'I can', 'you can', 'he can', 'we can', 'they can'... what is the infinitive? 'To can' doesn't sound quite right so we say the infinitive is 'to be able to' a bit of a mouthful to say the least and again the infinitive has little to do with the conjugations.

What is the point of me taking you on this little detour? It's to point out that you can use these conjugations seamlessly in your natural speech despite the fact you'd probably never even been aware that there was any discrepancy or flaunting of conjugation patterns going on. Not understanding why these forms are odd has never stopped you from being able to use them or made them seem in any way bizarre - or at least until I brought up the subject perhaps.

Similarly, if you're like me, you may well ask: 'but why do verbs have to conjugate and be so difficult?' And there is an answer. However, that answer will differ for every language, would involve an in-depth study of linguistics and history and will entirely distract you from learning and using the conjugations in the first place. So what's the solution to bypass this and cut to the chase?

For me, it's all about patterns. Thankfully most verbs in most languages conjugate much more neatly than the extreme examples I just gave you. All you really need to get going is the present tense.

Don't learn whole conjugations of verbs. Instead look for the patterns and commit to correcting irregular forms on the fly. For example, let me give you a mix of Spanish conjugations in the present tense - some regular, some irregular, but I'm sure you'll notice a pattern

- 1st person singular *tengo, vengo, veo, vuelvo*
- 2nd person singular *tienes, vienes, ves, vuelves*

- 1st person plural *tenemos, venimos, vemos, volvemos*

In the first person singular (or 'I'), you may notice all the verb forms end with an 'o'.

In the second person singular (or 'you'), you may notice all the verb forms end with an 'es'.

In the first person plural (or 'we'), you may notice all the verb forms end with an 'imos' or 'emos'.

You mostly don't need to learn each verb individually. Learn the basic patterns and you can go straight to speaking. So for example Spanish infinitives fall into one of three categories. Where English verbs are indicated by the preposition 'to' as in 'to sing', 'to dance', etc., Spanish infinitives end in either 'ar', 'er' or 'ir'.

Take a Spanish infinitive then, like *cantar* ('to sing') and in order to conjugate the first person or '**I**' form, you remove the '**ar**' leaving '*cant*' and add an "o" making the word *canto*, 'I' in Spanish is *yo* so *yo canto* means I sing.

This is pretty easy. Similarly in German, infinitives end in '-en' so *singen* is the infinitive of the verb 'to sing'. The present tense first person in German is just an 'e' so to conjugate the verb in German, we take the infinitive singen, remove the '-en' and add an '-e 'to get *singe*. 'I' in German is *Ich* so *Ich singe* means I sing.

Of course, there are exceptions and irregularities in all languages but the point is you want to initially (and initially only) ignore all that and cut everything down as much as possible to allow you to start talking. Once you get to the talking stage that's when you start concentrating on perfecting. If, on the other hand, you want to learn everything perfectly before you start talking so you won't make any mistakes and look silly, you will never start talking as it's only absorbing, listening and talking that will take you to the fluency stage.

6. PRESENT VERSUS PRESENT CONTINUOUS

There is a curious distinction in English that isn't found or used in most languages. You will at some point in your language learning come across a concept or quirk of grammar that doesn't exist in English and whilst initially being difficult to understand, it may make you ponder how it might feel to a native speaker to think this way.Here's an example in English.

Consider these two sentences :

'The man reads the book'

'The man is reading the book'

What is the difference? Both are in the present tense.

'The man reads the book' implies it's something he normally does or regularly does but he's not necessarily doing it right now. 'The man is reading the book' would imply he is doing it now or is in the middle of doing it. We naturally get this idea as native English speakers.

If I'm asked what I did yesterday I could say: 'well I'm reading the Lion, the Witch and the Wardrobe at the moment so yesterday I read a couple of chapters of that'. It is perfectly obvious to a native speaker that I'm not reading the book right now but that reading the book is an ongoing occurrence that I haven't completed yet.

Similarly, if I were asked, 'have you been to the shop yet?' the answer 'no it's raining' makes sense. The answer: 'No, it rains' makes a lot less sense.

Most other European languages don't have this distinction, or if they do, they don't implement it as rigidly as we do in English. In German for example there is no way to say 'I am working' you can only say 'I work'.

Spanish has both 'I work' and 'I'm working' but they are far more interchangeable than in English. The difference in English is about when it is happening and whether or not it is a regular occurrence versus a one-off event or an ongoing thing.

Think of it this way: every time someone new to English utters a sentence in the language, they have to decide whether the event is happening now, i.e. 'it's raining' is something frequent ('it rains in England'), or is an ongoing event, e.g. 'I'm reading a book about biology, I started it last year'. In the latter example it's not definite that I'm reading it right now, but if I said 'I can't answer the phone, I'm reading my book' it's fairly obvious I'm reading the book now. While that's quite a lot to consider every time you want to form a sentence in English, it's something native speakers do without even realising it because the difference in meaning is known instinctively but if you understand what is going on you can make the difference explicit. This concept I can imagine is fairly difficult to pick up as a foreign learner of English. Compare this difficulty with how easily you do it without even thinking about all the things your brain must be considering whilst choosing which of those expressions is best going to communicate what you have in mind. This is how a Spaniard feels using the subjunctive or a German putting the correct adjectival endings with nouns in a certain case because "it just sounds right".

7. PAST TENSES

How many past tenses does English have? It may have more than you thought! It may have even more than *I* thought, it has more than some languages and less than others. But why would we have more than one past tense? For the same reason we have a distinction between the present tense (*'I read'*) versus the present continuous (*'I am reading'*). They convey slightly different ideas. Other languages may convey the same ideas using marker words or it may just be inferred from the context. Come to think of it, this is quite a good description of what grammar is or does

- it's a way of coding or manipulating words to add or delineate meaning.

Getting back to English, I'm sure this is debatable but I'd say we have three standard past tenses in English. Allow me to explain them. If the idea of tenses has been an issue for you in the past when learning languages, just try to follow along. Don't try to memorise anything, just try and take it in.

The past tenses are:

The perfect

The simple past

The pluperfect

There are other past tenses in other languages. For example, Spanish and Italian have the imperfect tense and the meanings or functions between the languages overlap somewhat or are covered by other past tenses. Part of how the Spanish imperfect functions, for instance, is that it conveys something done habitually in the past, which is conveyed in English somewhat clumsily (in my opinion) as 'used to' as in 'I used to play the guitar'. In Spanish this sentence can be much more neatly rendered as *'tocaba la guitarra'*. This incorporates the meaning of 'used to play' (as opposed to 'played just once' which would use the preterite tense, or simple past as it's called in English). Meanwhile the past perfect or perfect tense is used to describe actions in the past that have been completed. In English, like in most European languages, it uses an auxiliary or "helping" verb, which just means we need two verbs together to make it.

In English, we make the perfect using the verb 'to have' and the past participle of the verb we want to use.

So for example if we took the present tense 'I eat' and put it in the perfect tense, it would become 'I *have eaten*'.

'I sing' would become 'I *have sung*',

'I danced' would become 'I *have danced*', etc., etc.

The simple past then is used to describe something in the past.

The perfect tense is used to describe something that happened in the near recent past.

Compare:

Simple past - 'I *ate* breakfast (yesterday)', with

Perfect tense – 'I *have* already *eaten* breakfast (this morning)'.

The pluperfect, which literally means "more than perfect" is like a double past tense that signifies something in the past happened before something else in the past.

For example: 'Brian had eaten all the chicken when Janet arrived home'.

Note: *'had'* and *'eaten'* are both forms of the past tense.

There is a lot more that can be said about the past tenses but this book is not the place and it wouldn't be beneficial to go into more detail. This is just a rough layman's guide. What I have laid out is just a rudimentary guide to sow some seeds in your mind that there is more than one past tense and the kind of different meanings they can convey.

The reason that further explanation isn't beneficial is I don't know which language you intend on learning and - as with most grammar - the tense, rules and meaning will change depending on which language it is that you are learning.

For example in Italian conversational speech (as opposed to a written book) they will almost exclusively use the perfect tense. Thus you will usually hear l'ho fatto ieri ("I've done it yesterday") rather than 'I did it yesterday'.

In conversational Spanish, especially in certain regions, they tend to use the preterite where the perfect would serve better. This is a little bit like the strange mix of tenses that happens in the south of the UK where you will quite often hear people saying 'I done it' instead of 'I did it' or 'I've done it', which seems a peculiar mix of simple and perfect in one hybrid tense.

8. FUTURE / CONDITIONAL

The future and conditional are pretty straightforward ideas though there are some worthy mentions. First of all, some languages don't have them but instead signal timeframes with marker words or solely through context. The future obviously informs us that an event will happen in the future; the conditional tense (as might be guessed) sets a conditional usually as an 'if' clause. If I won the lottery I would buy a new house.

Between the Germanic and Romance languages, there is a split in how the future and conditional are formed.

Germanic languages, like English and of course German form the future and the conditional by using a specific word.

Present Future Conditional

I sing I **will** sing I **would** sing

I sleep I **will** sleep I **would** sleep

I run I **will** run I **would** run

Romance languages are much neater and incorporate the whole meaning in one or two words.

The below examples are in Spanish

I sing - Canto : I will sing - Cantar**é** : I would sing - Cantar**í**a

I sleep - Duermo : I will sleep - Dormir**é** : I would sleep - Dormir**í**a

I run - Corro :I will run - Correr**é** : I would run - Correr**í**a

. . .

Talking about the future can be quite interesting. Some languages have a subjunctive tense, also often talked about as a mood. The basic idea of the subjunctive is it indicates doubt or lack of certainty. Again the exact usage of it in languages that have the subjunctive changes considerably. But essentially anything we say about the future isn't certain due to the very nature of time so there can often be quite a few quirks within languages when it comes to dealing with the future. Again I find these quirks fascinating, especially if they don't exist in English. If we revisit my earlier comment about grammar being a way to solve problems of expressing or delineating meaning this becomes quite an interesting point.

For example, in German there are three words for 'when'. If I wanted to talk about when I was young - something that is absolute and in the past - the word for when would be *als. Als ich jung war*, 'when I was young'. When talking about the future however the word would be, similarly to English *wenn* (unless you're asking a question in which case you would use the word *wann*). So *als, wenn* and *wann* can all be translated as 'when', but they are not interchangeable. They all signify something definitive either an event in the past, an event in the future or indicating a question.

Furthermore in German when you use the word *wenn*, it sends the verb to the end of the sentence. This is some major mind gymnastics if you haven't come across it before and to get my head around it I found it easier to make sentences up in English and apply the German rules to make the translation easier.

This would turn the normal English sentence 'I will buy a car when I <u>have</u> enough money' into 'I will buy a car when I enough money <u>have</u>'.

I used to regularly make these strange-sounding sentences up in my head throughout the day until it eventually became second nature, meaning I could in a split second render an English word order sentence into a more German order and then just translate the words and keep the word order. This was a good stepping stone for me and took a lot of stress out of speaking German with native speakers. After a while, it becomes unnecessary as you begin to think in German the translation function becomes obsolete unless you actually need to translate something. However in the interim period while I still had to work out what I wanted to say first in English it was a useful exercise.

In Romance languages, something interesting generally happens if you use the word *'when'* in a sentence and you are referring to the future.

In Spanish, if you use the word when referring to the future you have to use the subjunctive form of the verb after it.

In Italian, if you use the word 'when' in reference to the future you have to use the future form of the verb after it. Who knows why there is a difference? They have both come from the same original language: Latin. But there we have it. The important thing is to know that this kind of thing happens and find out what the rule is in your target language.

9. THE SUBJUNCTIVE

The subjunctive is something I have mainly encountered in Romance languages and as stated earlier expresses doubt or uncertainty. Again the rules and norms differ depending on which language you are learning. In German, it has its counterpart known as the Konjunktiv, which for the most part is used for reported speech.

In Spanish and Italian there are certain words that trigger the subjunctive and certain ideas can be expressed very well with it.

In Spanish you would say:

'I think he <u>has</u> a car'

*Creo que **tiene** un coche.*

This is a thought that you are asserting and so it is in the indicative mood, essentially the opposite of the subjunctive i.e. not expressing any doubt.

Compare this with the negative:

I don't think he <u>has</u> a car.

*No creo que **tenga** un coche*

Note in both the English sentences we say 'I think he **has**' and 'I don't think he **has**' - the conjugation of the verb 'to have' in the third person is always 'has'. In Spanish however, when we changed from positive asserting to negative introducing doubt the Spanish verb 'to have' in the third person shifts from *tiene* to *tenga*, this is the change from the indicative to the subjunctive.

In well-spoken Italian (although this is becoming less common in colloquial speech) both the negative and positive of this sentence would use the subjunctive to express doubt. I found this quite interesting when I first found out, having learned Spanish first I'd accepted the premise that thinking something made it certain and not thinking something made it uncertain hence indicative and subjunctive. However, when years later I learned Italian I had to re-evaluate it.

Italians would say:

'I think he has a car.'

*Penso che **abbia** una macchina.*

'I don't think he has a car.'

*Non penso che **abbia** una macchina*

. . .

Both are subjunctive and if you think about it - just because you think someone has a car doesn't mean they actually do. We routinely think things all the time that turn out to be wrong and the Italian language highlights this well by using the subjunctive in both cases. This led me to the great subjunctive thought experiment: if an Italian hears a Spaniard using the indicative 'I think he has a car', he must sound extremely confident of the fact? With the same logic if a Spaniard hears an Italian using the subjunctive 'I think he (subjunctive -might) have a car' he must sound very unconfident of the fact.

The subjunctive as with all grammar can give subtle clues and proffer extra information in a sentence that you might otherwise not pick up on.

Compare these two sentences:

*Quiero una casa que **tiene** una piscina* - Indicative

*Quiero una casa que **tenga** una piscina* – Subjunctive

This difference between these two sentences in Spanish is a little like the differences we went through when talking about definite and indefinite articles in English.

In both these sentences, the English translation would be the same, literally translated word for word we get

I want a house that **has** a swimming pool, but the *tiene/tenga* difference changes everything. Both words mean "has" because English doesn't really have a subjunctive. So what is the difference?

The first sentence using the indicative is referring to a house that must exist, i.e I have already seen the house and know it has a swimming pool, (either I've physically gone to see it or I've seen it on the television).

The second sentence using the subjunctive means the house doesn't actually exist, I want a house that has a swimming pool, it's an idea, I know a lot of houses have swimming pools, so there's a good chance of me getting one, but I'm not referring to a specific house that has a swimming pool, I'm just stating that I'd like the house I'm looking for to have a pool. The whole meaning of the sentence shifts just by swapping the mood of that one verb. Fascinating!

There is only one version of the subjunctive where the conjugation changes that springs to mind in the English language and it only happens with one verb. The example is 'If only I **were** rich'.

Normally 'were' is past tense, but here we are wishing we were rich now, not in the past. Furthermore, the correct past tense conjugation of the verb to be with 'I' would be 'I was' not 'I were'.

'Yesterday I won the lottery and I was rich' works but if I said 'yesterday I won the lottery and I were rich', it would just sound wrong, or very slangy at least. So what are we looking at here? This is in fact the last remnants of the subjunctive form in English. It is only noticeable with the verb 'to be' in the singular first and third persons.

Similarly 'I wish she were here with me', is the subjunctive, not a past tense. We know this as we are wishing now that she were here now, but the reason it is subjunctive is that despite our most ardent wishes the fact is she obviously isn't here with me or I wouldn't need to wish it.

Compare :

'She **was** here yesterday' – past tense indicative

'I wish she **were** here today' – present subjunctive

The subjunctive is found elsewhere in English but rather than a conjugation you will find the stem of the infinitive. For example:

'I insist that she **be** here at 11!'

Rather than 'I hope she **is** here at 11'.

10. THE IMPERATIVE

There is another mood, in addition to the indicative and the subjunctive. Don't panic this is a lot easier to get your head around. The imperative is basically just giving orders.

Stop!
Don't do that!
Help!

That kind of thing! There are rules in each language on how to take an infinitive and make out of it an imperative depending on who you are ordering to do something. This is something to bear in mind and understand but really it's infrequently used and you can pick it up later on. Still, it's a good seed to plant in your head now so you are aware that it exists and you can later look up how it is made in your target language.

11. PREPOSITIONS

Prepositions are another potentially huge topic. The very name "pre-position" or positioned in front is confusing, given that in many languages they end up at the end of the sentence. Prepositions are fickle things and tend to have little consistency across languages.

For example, for is an example of a preposition but in other languages, they don't use "for" in combination with *example*.

In Spanish they say por ejemplo however even though por sounds like for, it rarely means *for* when translated, por can mean by or because or through and a slew of other things.

In Italian the translation of for example is ad esempio where ad is the preposition *to*.

This is similar to German's zum Beispiel where zum is also the preposition *to*.

Some languages don't have prepositions at all, they use cases to mark words and some languages like German use a mix of prepositions and cases.

A basic list of prepositions in English to give you an idea would be: to, from, by, for, at, under, over, on, against etc etc you get the idea.

In a normal sentence you would expect to see them in front of their object for example

The cup was <u>on</u> *the table*. But compare that to the more complicated

The cup was <u>on top of</u> *the table*. What is the difference between the two? It's quite difficult to explain to a non native speaker.

Then we have times where a preposition gets mixed with a verb to create a phrasal verb. To pick someone is to choose someone but that is very different to picking someone up that could mean to lift them up or to collect them from somewhere.

Germanic languages tend to like phrasal verbs a lot and again the preposition used changes across the languages.

To switch off a light in German is to make the light out (Das Licht ausmachen)

Then in English, we have a mix of words we can't even decipher unless you know one of the Romance languages or Latin.

To admit comes from Latin you may recognise the ad part from our previous example ad esempio in Italian.

Admit comes from ad mittere with mittere meaning to send. Many English words begin with old Latin prepositions that don't even make sense in English, it is however interesting to deconstruct them to try and work out what they originally meant.

Some Latin prepositions contained in many English words

con (with) contain, consider, constitute, context

ad (to) admit, advertise, adventure, adversary

per (by/through) perspire, pertain, perfect, percussion

de (of/from) descend, despair, depend, derive

The list goes on and on. Some words even use multiple prepositions affixed to a noun such as condescend or con-de-scend with scend coming from scendere meaning to go down or get off in modern Italian.

You may have used the words pertain, contain, retain and maintain and never asked yourself what "tain" meant. Perhaps now you may feel curious? It's the curiosity that itches my language bug.

Similarly, we have Germanic mixes such as forget, forsake, forgo but we also have plenty of verbs where the preposition isn't glued to the word but actually floats around the sentence depending on usage.

. . .

For example "to take off". We could say "He took off his boots" which is already quite difficult for a foreign learner of English to work out the meaning. But most native speakers would render "He took off his boots" as the more colloquial "He took his boots off". In this sentence a foreign speaker has to know that the preposition off at the end of the sentence and thus annoyingly not prepositioned at all actually belongs to the verb "take" in this case. They have to know it and then mentally rejuggle it into a position next to the verb so they can translate the sentence in an easier way in their native language. We have a LOT of these kinds of verbs in English and I would imagine they are a nightmare for foreign learners of English everywhere.

Think of the difference between 'to take over' and 'to overtake' just for starters. Then we have to 'take up', 'to take down', 'to take issue with', 'to take the mick', 'to take on', 'to take off'… The list goes on and on and in many cases there's no way of looking at the verb and preposition to work out what the meaning is, and so these meanings just have to be learned.

For example 'to give up'. The meaning of this is obvious as a native speaker but if you think of each word literally 'give' and 'up' together you wouldn't assume they would mean 'to stop doing something'. Similarly unintuitive is 'to go off' as in 'the firework went off right next to me'. Why does 'went off', mean 'explode'? It's not something you could guess just by looking at the two words. Another example 'The cheese had gone off'. The two sentences use the same phrasal verb, but what does the explosion in the first have to do with mouldiness in the second? Consider yourself lucky you aren't learning English!

Getting back to word order, English may well be the master of preposition soup. I think I read a sentence once that ended in five prepositions - not bad for something that's very name suggests all five of them should be anywhere but at the end of the sentence.

From memory, the story goes something like this - little Johnny is in bed and his father comes up to ask him if he'd like a story. Johnny tells his dad there are two books on the table, a blue one and a pink one and he'd like to be read to from the blue one. His father goes downstairs, gets distracted and a few minutes later appears back in Johnny's room with the pink book under his arm, to which Johnny exclaims annoyed, 'What did you bring that book I didn't want to be read to out of up for!'

12. CASES

As we've already discussed, grammar is basically different solutions to encoding meaning into words. Some languages have come up with other systems and one of those systems is the case system, which you will find in Latin, Finnish, Russian, and also German. English too had a case system at one time but as with the pronoun 'thou' it was lost and today only a few vestiges of it remain.

As discussed nearer the beginning of this book, to get your head around the case system you need to understand sentence structure and (at the bare minimum) be able to identify subjects, direct objects and indirect objects. I will talk about cases using some German examples as German uses both cases and prepositions and also because we can pick out some vocabulary that is easily recognisable to English speakers so we won't get too lost.

The German cases are: Nominative, Accusative, Dative, Genitive.

Everything you say in German will use one of the four cases mentioned above.

The German words for 'a' and 'the' *inflect* or change depending on which of the four cases is being used. So what are the cases and how do we use them?

The most simplified explanation would be :

The Nominative case is used for sentence subjects.
The Accusative case is used for direct objects.
The Dative case is used for indirect objects.
The Genitive case is used to denote possession.

So how does this work in practice? First of all, a quick lesson in German... There are three genders in German - masculine, feminine and neuter - and then there are plurals.

Der Mann - the man
Die Frau - the woman
Das Mädchen - the girl

The plural for all three is also *die* as in *die Männer* ('the men'), d*ie Frauen* ('the women'), *die Mädchen* ('the girls').

All these words for 'the' are in the nominative form and are the words you would learn at GCSE level or high school level German. They generally don't teach the cases at this level in the UK as it's considered too complicated.

If the man is not the subject but the direct object then we have to change the word for 'the' accordingly, so for the sentence, 'I saw the man', the subject is me (I saw him), and the man, in this case, is a direct object (he is what is being seen).

The only change in German for the accusative case is essentially the masculine form which changes from *der* to *den*.

So in German, 'I see the man' becomes *Ich sehe den Mann.*

In the dative case all four of the words for 'the' change.

Der masculine becomes *dem.*
Die feminine becomes *der.*
Das neuter becomes *dem.*
Die plural becomes *den.*

Imagine now we are giving something to the man rather than seeing him. If you remember towards the beginning of this book I mentioned that we use the preposition *'to'* to mark the dative case in English indicating an indirect object. German uses a curious mix.

'I gave it **to** the man.'

*Ich gab es **zu dem** Mann*

Note that in English it is now the preposition *'to'* that marks the indirect object, whereas in German it is the fact that the word for *'the'* changes from *der* to *dem* that marks it. In fact, more often than not what you will actually see in German is not

*Ich gab es **zu** dem Mann* – but just

*Ich gab es **dem** Mann*

They no longer need to use the preposition as the case change is doing the marking.

Similarly, take 'I gave everything to the women' where 'the women' would be *die Frauen*. As the women are indirect objects in this case we put the word for 'the' *die* in the dative case which becomes *den*.

Ich gab alles zu den Frauen or *Ich gab alles den Frauen.*

Some prepositions in German trigger different cases depending on what you want to express. For example *'in'* + accusative case signifies movement whereas *'in'* + dative case signifies position.

For example *,die Kneipe* is 'the bar' as in, the place where you order a drink.

Ich gehe in <u>die</u> Kneipe 'I go <u>into</u> the bar.' It's **die** *Kneipe* (accusative) as I'm moving towards it. However, once I get there it's I*ch bin in **der** Kneipe* (I am <u>in</u> the bar), **der** *Kneipe* being appropriate as I'm now inside the bar.

We have the Genitive in English, although it's used slightly different than it is in German. For example, in the sentence 'my father's shoes' how many fathers are there? Just the one! That sneaky 's' on the end of 'father' is not a plural, but rather a genitive inflection we still have in English that denotes possession. We can also use it with names as in 'Ryan's book'. Note the *'s'* takes an apostrophe - while 'Ryans' would mean more than one Ryan, 'Ryan's' indicates some-thing that belongs to Ryan. Interesting how a little comma can completely change the meaning, and that's exactly what grammar is!

Finnish is a language I've been meaning to learn for a long time. It sounds amazing but as I've only been there once, and with work and family at that, I've just not had the time. I did make a start though and I love it! Finnish, like English, has no gender. Moreover, unlike English, there are also no words for 'a' or 'the'. Finnish gets around this and many other things with cases and suffixes. It's a fascinating language to me as it solves many many problems with the same solution: pop a suffix on the end to make your meaning clear. And with the absence of articles and gender despite its 15 different cases to German's four, it's still not that difficult to learn, (considering).

In Finnish, 'bus' is *bussi*. 'In the bus' would just be *bussissa*. 'By (the) bus' would be *bussilla*. By bus? ...as a question as in 'Did you go by bus?' would be *bussillako*? With *-illa* meaning 'by' and the *ko* suffix marking the fact that this is a question. It's a delightful building system and for me is the epitome of grammatical perfection, coding all the meaning into one sometimes fairly long word, and unpacking all the meanings is very fun to do too ...if you're into that kind of thing. It's like Lego for linguists!

Take this for an extreme example:

Bussi - bus
Bussi<u>ssa</u> - in the bus
Bussissa<u>mme</u> - in our bus
Bussissamme<u>kin</u> – in our bus as well
Bussissammekin<u>ko</u> – in our bus as well?

Honestly, I could just sit here and make up fantastic words all day!

A final note on cases...There is another place we can see the vestiges of cases and case markers in English and that is pronouns. These are like the archaeological remains of the once used English cases system. We already gave a worthy mention to the adjectival endings that marked case in 'wooden spoon' and 'golden egg' in the brief lesson in English grammar at the beginning of this book.

. . .

Pronouns have managed to stand the test of time and remain fairly intact in comparison to the few adjectives that hung on to their cases markings. If you think you don't understand cases and/or subjects and objects and you're a native English speaker, consider how you use pronouns instinctively and correctly. You do understand these concepts - if you didn't, you wouldn't be able to choose the right pronoun. Bringing fully into consciousness *why* you do it correctly may be tricky, but it's something you do understand at some deeper level!

Here's how the English pronouns stack up:

Nominative, Accusative, Dative, Genitive
I, me, (to) me, mine
you, you, (to) you, your(s)
{he/she/it}, {him/her/it}, (to) {him/her/it},
{his/her(s)/its}
we, us, (to) us, our(s)
they, them, (to) them, their(s)

The final (s) in the genitive is only used if the noun is omitted in English, for example

'It's her house, it's hers'

'It's our house, it's ours' etc.

Also, note how my/mine plays out the same way:

'It's my house, it's mine'

This actually matches quite closely with what German does in all sentences.

Ich sehe den Mann 'I see the man' reversed becomes *der Mann sieht mich* which is the same case change we see when we say 'I see her, she sees me'.

'*I* see **her**.'

In this example, 'I' is nominative as I am the subject of the first part of the sentence and 'her' is accusative as she is the direct object of the sentence.

'**She** sees **me**.'

However, when she sees me, 'she' changes from accusative 'her', to nominative 'she' as she is now the subject, and as I become the direct object 'I' becomes 'me'.

13. CLAUSES AND SUB-CLAUSES.

Clauses were explained to me as being the smallest part of a sentence that expresses a whole idea - or another way of explaining it is a unit of meaning that stands on its own.

For example 'Johnny sings' is a clause. You can say it on its own and everyone will understand you. 'In the morning' on its own, however, makes little sense. 'In the morning' would technically be classed as a phrase.

Put the two together and we have a sentence: 'Johnny sings in the morning'.

So far, so good. The reason I introduce this idea though is that some strange things can happen with clauses - for example, in the sentence 'I can't remember what happened' Can you say what function of grammar the word "what" is performing here?

'What' is in fact the subject of the sentence. This is a little confusing, even for me as I write it.

We can break the sentence up into a clause and a subclause, the clause being the main idea and the subclause being some add-on info.

(I can't remember) << main clause (what happened) << subclause. In the subclause, 'what' is the subject and 'happened' is the verb. Quite often when we have a clause and a subclause we will have a relative clause which will be introduced by a relative pronoun. These are 'that', 'who', 'whom', 'which', 'whose'.

'The boy that sang the song is brilliant.' If you analyse this sentence it's like double coding. What you are saying is: the boy is brilliant, that sang the song... but we have embedded the second idea into the middle of the first idea. Notice how the 'is' refers back to the boy, not the song. We don't read 'the song is brilliant' even though that is literally what the sentence says, our brains naturally and correctly understand that it is the boy that is brilliant. We see the word 'that', expect an injection of a new idea and remember the noun 'the boy' whilst parsing the next bit of the sentence 'sang the song' and remember that the end of the sentence 'is brilliant', refers to the boy. That's some mental gymnastics going on there and if no one has ever pointed it out to you, you were probably totally unaware that you even do this while reading!

The good news is, despite this being fairly complex to analyse consciously, we **do** normally do it without thinking and so you can often get away with just learning what the pronouns are in your target language and translating them as you would any other word. In some languages, such as German, however, you will need to understand this fairly well if you want to translate. And you will of course, once your mind gets over the shock, pick this up fairly quickly after seeing a few examples. This is how our brains actually work with languages, otherwise these kinds of grammar complexities wouldn't exist in the first place. Is it the so-called language instinct at play?

14. COMPARATIVES AND SUPERLATIVES.

These couldn't be easier to get a grip on and English is a great starting point if you're learning either a Germanic language or a Romance language as English (being a hybrid) contains both the versions you need to learn either.

We should know what an adjective is and be able to pick it out in a phrase like 'the house is big'. A comparative, meanwhile, does just that, compares it - 'the house is big, but the skyscraper is bigger' - and superlative sets the record essentially.

'The house is big, a skyscraper is bigger, but the Burj Khalifa is the biggest.'

This is what I'd refer to as the Germanic way to form them:

Big, bigger, the biggest
Tall, taller, the tallest
Round, rounder, the roundest, etc.

The Romance way to make them is as follows:

Beautiful, more beautiful, the most beautiful

So in Spanish we get *rápido, más rápido, el más rápido* (fast, more fast, the most fast)

In French we get *rapide, plus rapide, le plus rapide*

Whereas in German we get *schnell, schneller, am schnellsten* and in Dutch we get *snel, sneller, snelst*

Some very common adjectives can change quite dramatically, which usually means the words have been adapted from different roots at some point.

Take a look at 'good, better, the best'. Why don't we say 'good, gooder, the goodest'?

This change must have happened at some point before English and German became separate languages as the words are very similar in both and follow the same complete change.

Good, better, the best

Gut, besser, am besten

15. PRONUNCIATION

I'm obviously going to struggle a bit to write about pronunciation as I can write pretty much any group of letters in English and people can pronounce them in various ways. Some words can be pronounced correctly in multiple ways such as either/either and some words written the same way change from a verb to a noun depending on where you place the stress such as PERfect (noun) and PerFECT (verb) - and that's just in English!

Also, consider how differently these 3 words are pronounced despite the exact same spelling :

Comb Tomb Bomb

It's also been said the word "Ghoti" could be pronounced "fish" taking the 'gh' from 'enou**gh**', the 'o' from 'w**o**men' and the 'ti' from 'ac**ti**on'.

When discussing learning a foreign language and pronunciation it is useful however to make you aware of a few things, the first being very pertinent and important for you to bear in mind when trying to pronounce words in foreign languages:

If you've ever seen German written down, and I'm sure you have, you will have seen that some words carry an umlaut, the two dots over a vowel, such as *Mädchen* or **ü***ber*. If you ever wondered what these dots mean then you're about to find out. The umlaut is there to signify the change in vowel quality in that word. I'd never have thought that we had umlaut in English until I started learning A-level German at college and noticed something funny. Sometimes *Mädchen* was spelled *Mädchen* and sometimes as

Maedchen. Sometimes *über* was spelled *über* and other times as *ueber*. And sometimes *Köln* (Cologne' in German) was written *Köln* and other times as *Koeln*. I asked my teacher what was going on. What was explained to me was a bit of a revelation and also explains one of the main complaints I've heard from foreigners trying to learn English: 'Why does English have such a crazy spelling system?'

The explanation given to me for the different German spellings was that when typewriters and later keyboards came into common use they didn't have umlauts on them so the umlaut was written down as the sound is in German, i.e. ä – ae, ö – oe and ü – ue.

What has that got to do with English? Well, try saying the following words passing left to right.

Hat / Hate
Mat / Mate
Pet / Pete
Pin / Pine
Tot / Tote
Dot / Dote
Cut / Cute
Jut / Jute

Notice anything? It seems we have exactly the same system in English - the only difference is we put the 'e' at the end of the word instead of next to the vowel as is done in German. So in English, a final 'e' on the end of a word changes the sound of the preceding vowel. It also means that, as the final 'e' is providing a purely grammatical function, it itself is not pronounced, it is silent as it is a written tool to signify a vowel change to the reader, it is not part of the sound of the word itself. This obviously doesn't account for all of the quirks of English pronunciation, but it's a factor.

It in turn means that English speakers are not very good at pronouncing words that end in an 'e', especially when it comes to Romance languages such as Spanish and Italian.

For example, my wife's name is Teresa and this is shortened to Teré much like Peter is shortened to Pete or David to Dave only the final 'e' is pronounced in Spanish. (So imagine you are saying Te-re-sa - or Tay-ray-sah as it could be spelled to better show the pronunciation in Spanish - then imagine you just remove the last syllable so Te-re.) However, as we live in the UK at the moment most people just can't get their mouths to replicate this name so invariably people just call her Terry which ends not with the 'e' sound but an 'i' sound which is very common in English and hence easier to do for the local populace. While for an English speaker the difference may not be noticeable, for her it's huge as they are mispronouncing her name after all. Imagine taking an English name and swapping out the last vowel for another - say you're called Harry and everyone pronounced it Harro or Harra… it would be pretty noticeable.

Another feature of English is diphthongs. This is basically where two vowels are pronounced together, such as in 'haul'. If you say it and concentrate you should hear that you start the word with 'Ho' but it ends in an 'oo' sound before you finish on the 'l'.

The issue for English speakers is that most of our vowels are not true vowels as they are in Romance languages, but are in fact diphthongs.

Of the five vowels A E I O U in English, four of them are diphthongs.

If you consider the vowels as I was taught at primary school we would pronounce them like this 'a' is in cat, 'e' as in bet, 'i' as in bin, 'o' as in hot, 'u' as in umbrella where the vowel is pronounced as it sounds in the word that follows.

'a e i o u' as pronounced in the above words are all singular sounds

If we use those sounds to write the normally spoken vowels A E I O U we could write them thus:

A = e-i E = i I = a-i O = o-oo or o-u U = i-oo or i-u

Consider the word 'window'. It looks fairly innocent but if you say it a few times to yourself slowly you should notice that 'window' does not end in an 'oh' sound but glides from the 'oh' sound and actually ends in an 'oo' sound:

'Win-doh-oo'.

The summation of these pronunciation quirks in English leads many an English-speaking foreign language learner to innocently mangle words in other languages.

For example, *bene* in Italian will often be pronounced like the name Benny. This might not seem like a major offense to us but to an Italian it would sound like pronouncing 'carpet' as "keerpot".

Similarly, one of the most common pronunciation mistakes English speakers make when trying to impress Italians with their knowledge of the language is the pronunciation of the word *grazie*. Most English speakers will pronounce it like "gratsi", but the final 'e' in Italian is not silent but is actually there to indicate a plural and must be pronounced.

If you cast your mind back to 'How I learned Italian in a week' you will recall that feminine plurals in Italian get an 'e' so 1 *pizza*, 2 *pizze*. The same logic applies here. It's 1 grazia, 2 grazie (graces) so if you don't pronounce the final 'e' you're not just pronouncing it wrongly, you're not actually saying anything coherent at all.

To try and spell it phonetically as well as I can, *grazie* should be pronounced something like "grat-see-ey", *grazie* where both the final two vowels are pronounced as single separate sounds.

Similarly, the word *pero* ('but' in Spanish) shouldn't end in the same long gliding 'o' as we hear in the word 'window'. The best way to practice of course is speaking with native speakers and asking for corrections. If you speak enough your brain will tune in subconsciously to the sounds. Some people are better than others at this. For example, some people are brilliant at mimicking different accents at the drop of a hat. Don't worry, I'm one of those people who are terrible at imitating accents but that's because I've never immersed myself in the accents I've tried to mimic. It didn't stop me from learning Spanish nor having a good Spanish accent, it's just a question of putting the hours of practice in, the more intense and continuous the better.

CRITICAL MASS & THE 100TH MONKEY

I once read a fascinating report on the 100th Monkey Phenomenon. Researchers on the Japanese island of Koshima had begun leaving some food such as sweet potatoes out in the open for the local troop of Macaque monkeys. At some point, a female juvenile monkey figured out that she could remove the grit and sand on this new food source by taking it down to the water and washing it. As the now urban legend goes other juveniles began to copy her and one by one other monkeys learned to wash their potatoes. When however the number of monkeys washing their potatoes hit one hundred, something magical happened! Suddenly all the monkeys on the island began washing their potatoes, and not just on this island. Jumping natural barriers, monkeys on other islands began washing their potatoes too, seemingly without any interaction with the original potato dunkers. It was said that when the hundredth monkey began washing its potato some kind of critical mass was reached, instantly catapulting this new novel information across the whole collective consciousness of these primates.

While a lovely story, it has also been roundly debunked several times, so why am I telling you this? Unlike our spud-scrubbing friends, language acquisition takes place entirely in the confines of your own head. Being with a group of other learners isn't going to magically transfer any language into your head. The story does however nicely describe the idea of a critical mass and critical mass does come into language acquisition. You see, there is a lot to learn when you take on a new language. At the start of your journey learning your first new language, it will seem impossible, overwhelming even, and it will be hard to convince yourself that you will ever get there. As with the illusion of age, however, when you are five years old you think you will never be a grown-up, but once you hit adulthood the years melt away in retrospect and 30 to 40 seems to go by in a flash. The same is true for language learning. There is so much core language learning you need to do to get fluent, and yet the more of it you get through the less remains to be done and at the point where the balance tips and you have enough to speak and think in the language, the whole process speeds up exponentially.

The first language I really tried to get fluent in was Spanish. I'd already learned some German and French at school but I won't count that as it was more forced on me than done of my own volition. When I went to college I chose to learn Spanish and I wanted to get fluent. After several months in class, and despite not being bad at it I changed my outlook considerably. I came to the conclusion that I would never be fluent in Spanish as it was just too difficult to think in the language. I'd listen to some Spanish people having a conversation in Spanish, translate it to English, try and think of what I could say in Spanish that was relevant, and that I knew how to say... check my grammar, but by the time I'd done all that they'd already changed topic. I decided, a bit despondently, that I should adjust my aim and just try and get to the stage where I could say what I wanted as quickly as possible. It was around this time that I started making up my bad grammar English sentences to try and speed my translations up. I didn't have to do this at all when I was learning Italian. There was, as I stated in previous chapters, zero doubt I would become fluent. So what was the difference? Hindsight and experience mostly. But also I knew how to think in another language by that point. The mammoth task of learning enough of a new language to speak was tackled in just a few days. Apart from breaking the grammar down and knowing what questions to ask and what things I needed to be learning and what I should learn first, the greatest advantage Italian me had over Spanish me was that I could think straight away from day one with the Italian words I was learning - I didn't have to translate each sentence in my head. I learned the words and then when I heard them used or needed to use them myself, they were there in my head in Italian. I didn't start by thinking in English and trying to translate as I had done when getting to grips with Spanish. With Italian it was more like I had a small pool of vocabulary and verbs which I could think with and manipulate well enough to get across myriad meanings and as I did, I asked further questions and rephrased things such that my vocabulary increased naturally in conversation. If I needed to use a verb in Italian

I'd just think of the conjugation, not work it out like some mathematical formula.

The way critical mass works in language is two-fold. First off, as soon as you can talk and force yourself to only talk in the foreign language, your learning will accelerate. Rather than learning words from a book and looking them up in a dictionary, you will be learning them by asking in conversation what the word means and understanding the explanation, even if at the beginning you are having to ask two to three times till you get it. Secondly, once you have become fluent in your first foreign language, learning a third, fourth or even fifth will be easier as you can jump straight into thinking in the language.

When I sat down and learned 'fork', 'spoon', 'knife' and some simple verbs in Italian, I could think with them straight away, seeming to skip the need for mnemonics completely. My brain pretty much just mapped them where they needed to go. I made mistakes and mixed words up of course but my point is something like 95% of the difficulty of acquiring a new language was gone with Italian.

This is important to know, and any adult can grasp the aforementioned age example: time speeds up as you get older. An hour for a small child is an eternity, we've all experienced that, but for an adult sometimes several hours (or years) can fly by in seconds! This is also true of languages. If you want to crack it quickly, be confident, jump straight to knowing you will get there, don't let anything dissuade you from that idea and go at it like you mean it. You will find the same effect occurs. In the beginning, it will seem like you'll never get there, but it will happen so much quicker than you think if you go about it the right way and with the right mindset. The best tactic, if you can get yourself into a position that is practical, is to refuse to speak English at all while you are learning. Get yourself a tutor that will just speak to you in the target language and nothing else. Yes it's going to be a shock and excruciatingly difficult at first - expect some genuine headaches and setbacks - but that's life. Just plough on regardless and you will warp speed your way through the tough times I promise! The only thing really stopping anyone from learning their first foreign language in six months or less is first their level of belief and second the amount of time they can dedicate to it.

TERÉ & MEGAN

*M*y wife and I were in our late thirties when, faced with redundancy in my job in Belgium, I was offered the chance to avoid it by relocating to the UK. We didn't have any savings and there was a large pay rise on the cards if I took the opportunity so a few months later we loaded up the car and moved to the Midlands. My son didn't speak a word of English at this point and my wife spoke very little.

You've already learned how our son got on when we enrolled him at the local 'middle' school, but for my wife it was a very different experience. Stuck in the house in a strange country where her level of English wasn't realistically going to make her very employable, she decided to go and study. She enrolled on a fashion and design course at a local college. She'd always been interested in clothes and fashion and now she was going to learn how to design and make her own. The first day she came back she was very happy and excited. She hadn't understood much at all but it was a lot of practical work and the other students had been very nice to her in spite of the language barrier. After a few months she was chatting away in English and at the end of her first year, she'd taken driving lessons in English, passed her driving test, got herself a new career and bought herself a car.

My daughter Megan, from a previous relationship, came to live with me when she had just turned 18. Although I'd been back to see her religiously as often as possible while I'd been abroad, she was brought up in the UK. I'd just been transferred from Belgium to the UK for work and she'd been coming down to stay with my wife and I fairly regularly since I'd been back in the country.

She wanted to try living somewhere other than where she'd been brought up to meet new people and make new friends and have some new experiences, but more than anything she wanted to learn Spanish. Although my wife and I had been living in the UK for a year or so now, and despite the fact both my wife and son were now bi-lingual, we spoke mostly Spanish at home by force of habit.

The two situations were quite similar but with some big differences. My wife was obviously quite a bit older when she started learning English. She also wasn't really doing it by choice. Circumstances had forced our hand really and we were in the UK basically because the alternative was redundancy and a possible extended time trying to find a new job with a similar wage. I jumped at the chance of course. The chance to be closer to my daughter again, keep my job and career, and a salary increase to boot, it was a no-brainer, although not so much for my wife. She had family in Belgium, which is why we'd gone there in the first place, and we didn't know anyone in the Midlands at all. My wife was dropped into learning English at the deep end.

My daughter on the other hand was doing it purely out of preference. Whilst she was still young and could learn quickly I knew this could also backfire and I didn't want to see her have problems later on. So over a period of a few weeks, I tried my best to set expectations and explain how she might feel as she went through the process. Being sat around a table with people you know speaking a language you can't understand is pretty daunting, but if it goes on for prolonged periods you can feel pretty excluded and you can start to retract socially and I didn't want that to happen. My wife had been through this recently whilst studying and knew it wasn't much fun even with nice people. She'd got through it by concentrating on enjoying the practical parts of the course, designing clothes, picking colours and sorting through what kind of fabrics she'd like to use. Most of the conversation in the room was general chit-chat and of course all the other students wanted to learn Spanish which helped.

My wife and my daughter got on straight away and set up making word cards to stick around the house with words for things like 'fridge' and 'window' in both languages to stick all around the house.

Teré and Megan would chat away and help each other with vocab and expressing ideas. After a few months, Megan had saved up some money and went and did a two week course in Valencia, Spain. She learned Spanish at a language school there and came back enthused!

Both my ladies learned to be conversant in their first foreign language pretty much from scratch in under a year. How did they do it? They both sorted out their "why", which was different in each case. My wife, now living in England, didn't have much choice but to try and learn the language as it was a necessary step if she wanted any kind of a life here. Her husband was English and our son quickly became bilingual. Radio and television were in English and she quickly became immersed in the language, like it or not. My daughter had come out to see us in Spain when we lived there and we'd been going to visit her regularly in the UK so she'd often heard us speaking in Spanish. Naturally she wanted to learn it and so she put herself in a position where she'd hear it day in and day out.

It can't have been easy for either of them. Don't let me make you imagine there is an easy way to learn languages - there isn't. But there *is* a quick way! Learning languages is uncomfortable. Learning it quickly makes the uncomfortableness more intense, but then you get through it quicker. It's a trade off, as many things in life are. However, age or location has nothing to do with your failure. If you think you're too old, or you can't move to the country where the language you want to learn is spoken, these are excuses and are highlighting to you that your "why" isn't strong enough or well defined enough. For every reason you think you can't learn a language, write down ten better reasons why you can. Anyone can do it with the right "why", the right mindset and choosing the right conditions!

HELPFUL THINGS TO ASK YOURSELF ABOUT YOUR TARGET LANGUAGE

*I*n my outline of how I went about learning Italian in a week, I spoke of various things I knew I needed to learn to get to the speaking stage as quickly as possible. I will detail some of these here. Again, they will be based around the European languages that I know, and even with regard to them it's not a comprehensive list, as no doubt I'm doing some things unconsciously. There are also things in some languages I'm not aware of. Even in the recent past when I started learning Dutch, which is very similar to both German and English at the macro level, at the micro level it was full of little details and nuances that I had not come across or considered before. But this list will give you a good starting point to build from at the very least and consists of the first questions I ask of anyone that speaks a language that I don't when I try and find out how their language hangs together as I genuinely find it fascinating.

WHAT TO ASK YOURSELF:

Is the language written phonetically (i.e, written as it sounds)?

What is the normal sentence structure? (e.g. Subject,Verb,Object)?

Does the language have gendered nouns?

How are plurals made?

Do adjectives go before or after the noun?

How many tenses does the language have and what are they?

Is there a subjunctive? How do you make it?

Is there a conditional/future tense? How is it used? Word order?

Is there a case system in the language or articles or both?

Does the language use marker words, if so for what functions?

What are the basic question words ('how many', 'what', 'who', 'when', 'how' etc.)?

What ways are there to make a question (inversion, suffixes, other)?

Are there any patterns in the verb conjugations that can help me learn them? (I'd actually ask 'how are the verbs conjugated?' as, generally speaking, mother-tongue speakers won't have a clue what patterns there are. That's up to you to notice.)

CONCLUSION

*O*f course, I'm not about to suggest that anyone can go and learn enough of a foreign language in 5 or 6 days to hold a conversation. Not if it's your first time learning one. What I am saying is that if you fix your mindset, commit to a lifelong journey and embrace your mistakes and the whole experience, everything about learning a language becomes a pleasure and rewarding in and of itself. Even the discomfort of not understanding or embarrassment when making a mistake are signs of growth, not failure. When I make a mistake, even if it's in English, the feeling of embarrassment is by now a faint background emotion I'm aware of. I can know I'm feeling embarrassed but it's not something that causes me any physical effects as it did when I was young. We grow as people and mature, which is why I say if you have the mindset for it, everything will push you forward rather than pull you back. In the argument between the optimist and the pessimist, they are both right according to their world views. The question is: what do you want to focus on? That's not to say be blindly oblivious to problems, but rather be aware of them and confront them. Expect the best; prepare for the worst.

If you have already struggled along and learned your first foreign language and got to a decent level of fluency, go ahead and learn another. You already have most of the tools you need. The process is ridiculously easier the second time around.

If you're about to learn your first foreign language, I highly recommend finding someone that knows the language who can help explain what you need to understand about English first. When you approach it this way, once you start learning your target language you will be coming at it knowing how much of it is similar to English and just noting the few differences here and there that you may need to tweak, rather than climbing the mountain of obstacles presented in trying to learn a new language and at the same time learning grammar. Don't look for books teaching English grammar as generally what you will get is books on punctuation and when to use capitals. You may have noticed I'm no expert there. You need someone who can explain English grammar to you from a language point of view, and someone who has been through the journey of learning a foreign language is probably the best person to help you get the job done. Note that someone who was brought up bilingual will probably be as clueless as you about grammar so don't let the fact that they can dazzle you in another tongue make you think they understand languages - that's a whole different ball game.

If you're still not convinced about the grammar part of things, dwell a little on the section where we covered the passive voice and the vase that was mysteriously knocked over. Understanding grammar and how it works means you get more meaning out of every sentence uttered. You can infer things, for instance, that other people wouldn't think of. And if you're a salesman, a good grasp of grammar is insanely effective when it comes to getting sales and pre-empting objections - just by building your sentences in a certain way and observing how your customer is unconsciously building theirs can be enough to give you an upperhand. Approach grammar with the view of understanding what it does and what it will enable you to do, not as a list of chores. The "why" of grammar is that it's the key that unlocks language, both in your mother tongue and all other languages. It opens the doorway to a flood of information. You will see words in English and be able to unpack them to get new meaning out of them. You will be able to scan sentences in languages you've never seen or learned before and work out what certain words are doing, even if you don't know what the words mean! Once you have your "why" firmly fixed, the reason to learn conjugations becomes obvious - it becomes fun, a joy even rather than a chore because it's moving you towards your goal of communicating in another language. This is why it's taught wrongly in formal language courses: they don't start with a good enough why. In fact, they skip that part entirely.

Consider your "WHY". Why do you want to learn a language? Envisage what you will feel like and what you will do once you are fluent. How will people react to you and look at you and where will you be able to go and what could you do? Mentally prepare yourself for a long and rewarding journey of discovery, friend making, philosophy and history. Enjoy your mistakes too - laugh at yourself and your attempts to speak another language as you would laugh at a small child saying funny things when they first start talking. Immerse yourself in the words and rhythms and do it every day! Make a start, find out a few of the basics of the language and then jump into speaking it as soon as possible. Leave as much of the grammar as is practical till later in your learning adventure. You will need at least vocab and basic verb conjugations in the present tense to start with but leave it there. Don't get bogged down in grammar, don't learn every conjugation for every verb. Just find out what the most used ones are, learn a handful every day and save the hardcore grammar for when you are already getting up to speed with speaking. The grammar outlined in this book is critical for fluency, but so is not learning it by rote right from the start. Pick your approach wisely! Learning a language is a lifestyle choice, not a whim. So make a decision, pick your language and get practising. Spend your time in the language, not on it!

REVIEW

If you've enjoyed this book please click the link below which will redirect you to the Amazon store in your country (amazon.com, amazon.co.uk, etc.) and leave a review.

Your review helps other readers find this book in the Amazon store and provides valuable feedback for the author.

US: https://www.amazon.com/review/create-review/?ie=UTF8&channel=glance-detail&asin=B09NRHG649

UK: https://www.amazon.co.uk/review/create-review/?ie=UTF8&channel=glance-detail&asin=B09NRHG649

You can modify the above links for your country by swapping out the .com for whatever you country uses e.g .es for Spain etc.

Many thanks

ACKNOWLEDGMENTS

Resources:

Babbel.com. (n.d.). 10 Tips To Learn Any Language From An Expert. Babbel Magazine. Retrieved 20 February 2021, from https://www.babbel.com/en/magazine/10-tips-from-an-expert

D., S. (2021, January 26). How Polyglots Learn Languages and Stay Sane: Gems of Wisdom from 10 of the Best. FluentU Language Learning. https://www.fluentu.com/blog/how-polyglots-learn-language/

Lewis, B. (2020, November 29). How to become a polyglot. Fluent in 3 Months - Language Hacking and Travel Tips. https://www.fluentin3months.com/how-to-become-a-polyglot/

Neil, S. (2018, October 27). 10 Oldest Bridges in the World. Oldest.Org. https://www.oldest.org/structures/bridges/

VOA Learning English. (2017, November 14). Pig or Pork? Cow or Beef? VOA. https://learningenglish. voanews.com/a/words-and-their-stories-pig-or-pork-cow-or-beef/4104856.html

Wikipedia contributors. (2020, September 10). List of English words with dual French and Anglo-Saxon variations. Wikipedia. https://en.wikipedia.org/ wiki/ List_of_English_words_with_dual_French_and_An glo-Saxon_variations

Wikipedia contributors. (2021, January 5). Hello. Wikipedia. https://en.wikipedia.org/wiki/Hello

Wikipedia contributors. (2021, June 5). Spaced repe-tition. Wikipedia. https://en.wikipedia.org/ wiki/Spaced_repetition

U. (2021, April 25). The Order of Finnish Suffixes - Miehelleni Talossammekin. Uusi Kielemme. https:// uusikielemme.fi/finnish-grammar/the-order-of-finnish-suffixes

Wikipedia contributors. (2021a, May 31). List of tallest buildings. Wikipedia. https://en.wikipedia. org/wiki/List_of_tallest_buildings

Change the stress, change the meaning: 35 words that change meaning. (n.d.). EngVid. Retrieved 6 June 2021, from https://www.engvid.com/english-resource/35-words-stress-changes-meaning/

Change the stress, change the meaning: 35 words that change meaning. (n.d.). EngVid. Retrieved 6 June 2021, from https://www.engvid.com/english-resource/35-words-stress-changes-meaning/

The Hundredth Monkey Phenomenon. (n.d.). Hilo.Hawaii.Edu. Retrieved 6 June 2021, from https://hilo.hawaii.edu/%7Eronald/HMP.htm

U. (2021, April 25). *The Order of Finnish Suffixes - Miehelleni Talossammekin.* Uusi Kielemme. https://uusikielemme.fi/finnish-grammar/the-order-of-finnish-suffixes

Burden, D. (2014, September 20). *Missing 'S' in French words.* WordReference Forums. https://forum.wordreference.com/threads/missing-s-in-french-words.158706/

Pronouns: Three Cases. (n.d.). Web.Ku.Edu. Retrieved 6 June 2021, from https://web.ku.edu/%7Eedit/pronouns.html

G. (2020, January 14). German Umlauts. Study in
Germany   for   Free.   https://www.studying-in-
germany.org/german-umlauts/#:%7E:text=
Umlauts%20are%20assimilations%20or%20vowel

Meditation for Spanish Learners: Teach Yourself Spanish
Whilst Relaxing, Book 1 - Los Números (1-10)

Meditation for Spanish Learners: Teach Yourself Spanish
Whilst Relaxing, Book 2 - Los Números (10-20)

Meditation for Spanish Learners: Teach Yourself Spanish
Whilst Relaxing: Book 3 - Los Números (20-100)